Life of
CHOPIN

Life of
CHOPIN

FRANZ LISZT

DOVER PUBLICATIONS, INC.
Mineola, New York

Bibliographical Note

This Dover edition, first published in 2005, is an unabridged republication of the work originally published by Oliver Ditson and Company, Boston, c. 1863. Martha Walker Cook translated the work from the original French.

Library of Congress Cataloging-in-Publication Data

Liszt, Franz, 1811–1886.
    [F. Chopin. English]
    Life of Chopin / Franz Liszt.
        p. cm.
    "Martha Walker Cook translated the work from the original French"—
T.p. verso.
    Originally published: 4th ed. rev. Boston : Oliver Ditson, 1863?
    ISBN-13: 978-0-486-44625-7 (pbk.)
    ISBN-10: 0-486-44625-5 (pbk.)
    1. Chopin, Frâdâric, 1810–1849. 2. Composers—Biography. I. Cook,
Martha Walker, 1806–1874. II. Title.

ML410.C54L734 2006
786.2'092—dc22
[B]

                        2005052034

Manufactured in the United States by LSC Communications
44625508   2019
www.doverpublications.com

Contents

Contents

DEDICATION OF THE TRANSLATION
TO JAN PYCHOWSKI

Without your consent or knowledge, I have ventured to dedi-
cate this translation to you!

As the countryman of Chopin, and filled with the same
earnest patriotism which distinguished him; as an impassioned
and perfect Pianist, capable of reproducing his difficult compositions in all the subtle tenderness, fire, energy, melancholy,
despair, caprice, hope, delicacy and startling vigor which they
imperiously exact; as thorough master of the complicated
instrument to which he devoted his best powers; as an erudite
and experienced possessor of that abstruse and difficult science,
music; as a composer of true, deep, and highly original genius—
this dedication is justly made to you!

Even though I may have wounded your characteristically
haughty, shrinking, and Slavic susceptibilities in rendering so
public a tribute to your artistic skill, forgive me! The high moral
worth and manly rectitude which distinguish you, and which
alone render even the most sublime genius truly illustrious in
the eyes of woman, almost force these inadequate and imperfect
words from the heart of the translator.

M. W. C.

PREFACE

TO a people, always prompt in its recognition of genius, and ready to sympathize in the joys and woes of a truly great artist, this work will be one of exceeding interest. It is a short, glowing, and generous sketch, from the hand of Franz Liszt, (who, considered in the double light of composer and performer, has no living equal,) of the original and romantic Chopin; the most ethereal, subtle, and delicate among our modern tone-poets. It is a rare thing for a great artist to write on art, to leave the passionate worlds of sounds or colors for the colder realm of words; rarer still for him to abdicate, even temporarily, his own throne, to stand patiently and hold aloft the blazing torch of his own genius, to illume the gloomy grave of another: yet this has Liszt done through love for Chopin.

It is a matter of considerable interest to note how the nervous and agile fingers, accustomed to sovereign rule over the keys, handle the pen; how the musician feels as a man; how he estimates art and artists.

Liszt is a man of extensive culture, vivid imagination, and great knowledge of the world; and, in addition to their high artistic value, his lines glow with poetic fervor, with impassioned eloquence. His musical criticisms are refined and acute, but without repulsive technicalities or scientific terms, ever sparkling with the poetic ardor of the generous soul through which the discriminating, yet appreciative awards were poured. Ah! in these days of degenerate rivalries and bitter jealousies, let us welcome a proof of affection so tender as his *Life of Chopin!*

It would be impossible for the reader of this book to remain ignorant of the exactions of art. While, through its eloquence and subtle analysis of character, it appeals to the cultivated literary tastes of our people, it opens for them a dazzling perspective into that strange world of tones, of whose magical realm they know, comparatively speaking, so little. It is intelligible to all who think or feel; requiring no knowledge of music for its comprehension.

The compositions of Chopin are now the mode, the rage. Everyone asks for them, everyone tries to play them. We have, however, but few remarks upon the peculiarities of his style, or the proper manner of producing his works. His compositions, generally perfect in form, are never abstract conceptions, but had their birth in his soul, sprang from the events of his life, and are full of individual and national idiosyncrasies, of psychological interest. Liszt knew Chopin both as man and artist; Chopin loved to hear him interpret his music, and himself taught the great Pianist the mysteries of his undulating rhythm and original *motifs*. The broad and noble criticisms contained in this book are absolutely essential for the musical culture of the thousands now laboriously but vainly struggling to perform his elaborate works, and who, having no key to their multiplied complexities of expression, frequently fail in rendering them aright.

And the masses in this country, full of vivid perception and intelligent curiosity, who, not playing themselves, would yet fain follow with the heart compositions which they are told are of so much artistic value, will here find a key to guide them through the tuneful labyrinth. Some of Chopin's best works are analyzed herein. He wrote for the *heart of his people*; their joys, sorrows, and caprices are immortalized by the power of his art. He was a strictly national tone-poet, and to understand him fully, something must be known of the brave and haughty, but unhappy country which he so loved. Liszt felt this, and has been exceedingly happy in the short sketch given of Poland. We actually know more of its picturesque and characteristic customs after a perusal of his graphic pages, than after a long course of dry historical details. His remarks on the Polonaise and Mazourka are full of the philosophy and essence of history. These dances grew directly from the heart of the Polish people; repeating the martial valor and haughty love of noble exhibition of their men; the tenderness, devotion, and subtle coquetry of their women— they were of course favorite forms with Chopin; their national character made them dear to the national poet. The remarks of Liszt on these dances are given with a knowledge so acute of the traits of the nation in which they originated, with such a gorgeousness of description and correctness of detail that they rather resemble a highly finished picture, than a colder work of words only. They have all the splendor of a brilliant painting. He seizes the secrets of the nationality of these forms, traces them through the heart of the Polish people, follows them through their marvelous transfiguration in the pages of the Polish artist, and reads by their light much of the sensitive and exclusive character of Chopin, analyzing it with the skill of love, while depicting it with romantic eloquence.

To those who can produce the compositions of Chopin in the spirit of their author, no words are necessary. They follow with the heart the poetic and palpitating emotions so exquisitely wrought through the aerial tissue of the tones by this "subtle-souled Psychologist," this bold and original explorer in the invisible world of sound;—all honor to their genius:

> "Oh, happy! and of many millions, they
> The purest chosen, whom Art's service pure
> Hallows and claims—whose hearts are made her throne,
> Whose lips her oracle, ordained secure,
> To lead a priestly life, and feed the ray
> Of her eternal shrine, to them alone
> Her glorious countenance unveiled is shown:
> Ye, the high brotherhood she links, rejoice
> In the great rank allotted by her choice!
> The loftiest rank the spiritual world sublime,
> Rich with its starry thrones, gives to the sons of Time!"
>
> *Schiller.*

Short but glowing sketches of Heine, Meyerbeer, Adolphe Nourrit, Hiller, Eugène Delacroix, Niemcevicz, Mickiewicz, and Madame Sand, occur in the book. The description of the last days of poor Chopin's melancholy life, with the untiring devotion of those around him, including the beautiful countess, Delphine Potocka; his cherished sister, Louise; his devoted friend and pupil, M. Gutman, with the great Liszt himself, is full of tragic interest.

No pains have been spared by the translator to make the translation acceptable, for the task was truly a labor of love. No

motives of interest induced the lingering over the careful rendering of the charmed pages, but an intense desire that our people should know more of musical art; that while acknowledging
the generosity and eloquence of Liszt, they should learn to
appreciate and love the more subtle fire, the more creative
genius of the unfortunate, but honorable and honored artist,
Chopin.

Perchance Liszt may yet visit us; we may yet hear the match-
less Pianist call from their graves in the white keys, the delicate
arabesques, the undulating and varied melodies, of Chopin. We
should be prepared to appreciate the great Artist in his enthusiastic rendering of the master-pieces of the man he loved; prepared to greet him when he electrifies us with his wonderful
Cyclopean harmonies, written for his own Herculean grasp,
sparkling with his own Promethean fire, which no meaner hand
can ever hope to master! "Hear Liszt and die," has been said by
some of his enthusiastic admirers—understand him and live,
were the wiser advice!

In gratitude then to Chopin for the multiplied sources of high
and pure pleasure which he has revealed to humanity in his creations, that human woe and sorrow become pure beauty when
his magic spell is on them, the translator calls upon all lovers of
the beautiful "to contribute a stone to the pyramid now rapidly
erecting in honor of the great modern composer"—ay, the living
stone of appreciation, crystalized in the enlightened gratitude of
the heart.

"So works this music upon earth
God so admits it, sends it forth,
To add another worth to worth—

A new creation-bloom that rounds
The old creation, and expounds
His Beautiful in tuneful sounds."

CHAPTER I.

DEEPLY regretted as he may be by the whole body of
artists, lamented by all who have ever known him, we must
still be permitted to doubt if the time has yet arrived in
which he, whose loss is so peculiarly deplored by ourselves, can
be appreciated in accordance with his just value, or occupy that
high rank which in all probability will be assigned him in the
future.

If it has been often proved that "no one is a prophet in his
own country"; is it not equally true that the prophets, the men
of the future, who feel its life in advance, and prefigure it in
their works, are never recognized as prophets in their own
times? It would be presumptuous to assert that it can ever be
otherwise. In vain may the young generations of artists protest
against the "Anti-progressives," whose invariable custom it is to
assault and beat down the living with the dead: time alone can
test the real value, or reveal the hidden beauties, either of musical compositions, or of kindred efforts in the sister arts.

As the manifold forms of art are but different incantations,
charged with electricity from the soul of the artist, and destined
to evoke the latent emotions and passions in order to render
them sensible, intelligible, and, in some degree, tangible; so
genius may be manifested in the invention of new forms, adapted, it may be, to the expression of feelings which have not yet
surged within the limits of common experience, and are indeed
first evoked within the magic circle by the creative power of
artistic intuition. In arts in which sensation is linked to emotion,
without the intermediate assistance of thought and reflection,
the mere introduction of unaccustomed forms, of unused modes,

1

must present an obstacle to the immediate comprehension of any very original composition. The surprise, nay, the fatigue, caused by the novelty of the singular impressions which it awakens, will make it appear to many as if written in a language of which they were ignorant, and which that reason will in itself be sufficient to induce them to pronounce a barbarous dialect. The trouble of accustoming the ear to it will repel many who will, in consequence, refuse to make a study of it. Through the more vivid and youthful organizations, less enthralled by the chains of habit; through the more ardent spirits, won first by curiosity, then filled with passion for the new idiom, must it penetrate and win the resisting and opposing public, which will finally catch the meaning, the aim, the construction, and at last render justice to its qualities, and acknowledge whatever beauty it may contain. Musicians who do not restrict themselves within the limits of conventional routine, have, consequently, more need than other artists of the aid of time. They cannot hope that death will bring that instantaneous *plus-value* to their works which it gives to those of the painters. No musician could renew, to the profit of his manuscripts, the deception practiced by one of the great Flemish painters, who, wishing in his lifetime to benefit by his future glory, directed his wife to spread abroad the news of his death, in order that the pictures with which he had taken care to cover the walls of his studio, might suddenly increase in value!

Whatever may be the present popularity of any part of the productions of one, broken by suffering long before taken by death, it is nevertheless to be presumed that posterity will award to his works an estimation of a far higher character, of a much more earnest nature, than has hitherto been awarded them. A high rank must be assigned by the future historians of music to one who distinguished himself in art by a genius for melody so rare, by such graceful and remarkable enlargements of the harmonic tissue; and his triumph will be justly preferred to many of far more extended surface, though the works of such victors may be played and replayed by the greatest number of instruments, and be sung and resung by passing crowds of *Prime Donne*.

In confining himself exclusively to the Piano, Chopin has, in our opinion, given proof of one of the most essential qualities of a composer—a just appreciation of the form in which he possessed the power to excel; yet this very fact, to which we attach so much importance, has been injurious to the extent of his fame. It would have been most difficult for any other writer, gifted with such high harmonic and melodic powers, to have resisted the temptation of the *singing* of the bow, the liquid sweetness of the flute, or the deafening swells of the trumpet, which we still persist in believing the only fore-runner of the antique goddess from whom we woo the sudden favors. What strong conviction, based upon reflection, must have been requisite to have induced him to restrict himself to a circle apparently so much more barren; what warmth of creative genius must have been necessary to have forced from its apparent aridity a fresh growth of luxuriant bloom, unhoped for in such a soil! What intuitive penetration is revealed by this exclusive choice, which, wresting the different effects of the various instruments from their habitual domain, where the whole foam of sound would have broken at their feet, transported them into a sphere, more limited, indeed, but far more idealized! What confident perception of the future powers of his instrument must have presided over his voluntary renunciation of an empiricism, so widely spread, that another would have thought it a mistake, a folly, to have wrested such great thoughts from their ordinary interpreters! How sincerely should we revere him for this devotion to the Beautiful for its own sake, which induced him not to yield to the general propensity to scatter each light spray of melody over a hundred orchestral desks, and enabled him to augment the resources of art, in teaching how they may be concentrated in a more limited space, elaborated at less expense of means, and condensed in time!

Far from being ambitious of the uproar of an orchestra, Chopin was satisfied to see his thought integrally produced upon the ivory of the key-board; succeeding in his aim of losing nothing in power, without pretending to orchestral effects, or to the brush of the scene-painter. Oh! we have not yet studied with sufficient earnestness and attention the designs of his delicate pencil, habituated as we are, in these days, to consider only those composers worthy of a great name, who have written at least half-a-dozen Operas, as many Oratorios, and various Symphonies:

vainly requiring every musician to do every thing, nay, a little more than everything. However widely diffused this idea may be, its justice is, to say the least, highly problematical. We are far from contesting the glory more difficult of attainment, or the real superiority of the Epic poets, who display their splendid creations upon so large a plan; but we desire that material proportion in music should be estimated by the same measure which is applied to dimension in other branches of the fine arts; as, for example, in painting, where a canvas of twenty inches square, as the *Vision of Ezekiel,* or *Le Cimetière* by Ruysdaël, is placed among the chefs d'œuvre, and is more highly valued than pictures of a far larger size, even though they might be from the hands of a Rubens or a Tintoret. In literature, is Beranger less a great poet, because he has condensed his thoughts within the narrow limits of his songs? Does not Petrarch owe his fame to his *Sonnets*? and among those who most frequently repeat their soothing rhymes, how many know anything of the existence of his long poem on Africa? We cannot doubt that the prejudice which would deny the superiority of an artist—though he should have produced nothing but such Sonatas as Franz Schubert has given us—over one who has portioned out the insipid melodies of many Operas, which it were useless to cite, will disappear; and that in music, also, we will yet take into account the eloquence and ability with which the thoughts and feelings are expressed, whatever may be the size of the composition in which they are developed, or the means employed to interpret them.

In making an analysis of the works of Chopin, we meet with beauties of a high order, expressions entirely new, and a harmonic tissue as original as erudite. In his compositions, boldness is always justified; richness, even exuberance, never interferes with clearness; singularity never degenerates into uncouth fantasticalness; the sculpturing is never disorderly; the luxury of ornament never overloads the chaste eloquence of the principal lines. His best works abound in combinations which may be said to form an epoch in the handling of musical style. Daring, brilliant and attractive, they disguise their profundity under so much grace, their science under so many charms, that it is with difficulty we free ourselves sufficiently from their magical enthrallment, to judge coldly of their theoretical value. Their worth has, however, already been felt; but it will be more highly estimated when the time arrives for a critical examination of the services rendered by them to art during that period of its course traversed by Chopin.

It is to him we owe the extension of chords, struck together in arpeggio, or *en batterie*; the chromatic sinuosities of which his pages offer such striking examples; the little groups of super-added notes, falling like light drops of pearly dew upon the melodic figure. This species of adornment had hitherto been modeled only upon the *Fioritures* of the great Old School of Italian song; the embellishments for the voice had been servilely copied by the Piano, although become stereotyped and monotonous: he imparted to them the charm of novelty, surprise and variety, unsuited for the vocalist, but in perfect keeping with the character of the instrument. He invented the admirable harmonic progressions which have given a serious character to pages, which, in consequence of the lightness of their subject, made no pretension to any importance. But of what consequence is the subject? Is it not the idea which is developed through it, the emotion with which it vibrates, which expands, elevates and ennobles it? What tender melancholy, what subtlety, what sagacity in the master-pieces of La Fontaine, although the subjects are so familiar, the titles so modest? Equally unassuming are the titles and subjects of the *Studies* and *Preludes*; yet the compositions of Chopin, so modestly named, are not the less types of perfection in a mode created by himself, and stamped, like all his other works, with the high impress of his poetic genius. Written in the commencement of his career, they are characterized by a youthful vigor not to be found in some of his subsequent works, even when more elaborate, finished, and richer in combinations; a vigor, which is entirely lost in his latest productions, marked by an over-excited sensibility, a morbid irritability, and giving painful intimations of his own state of suffering and exhaustion.

If it were our intention to discuss the development of Piano music in the language of the Schools, we would dissect his magnificent pages, which afford so rich a field for scientific observation. We would, in the first place, analyze his *Nocturnes*,

Ballades, Impromptus, Scherzos, which are full of refinements of harmony never heard before; bold, and of startling originality. We would also examine his *Polonaises, Mazourkas, Waltzes* and *Boleros.* But this is not the time or place for such a study, which would be interesting only to the adepts in Counterpoint and Thoroughbass.

It is the feeling which overflows in all his works, which has rendered them known and popular; feeling of a character eminently romantic, subjective individual, peculiar to their author, yet awakening immediate sympathy; appealing not alone to the heart of that country indebted to him for yet one glory more, but to all who can be touched by the misfortunes of exile, or moved by the tenderness of love.

Not content with success in the field in which he was free to design, with such perfect grace, the contours chosen by himself, Chopin also wished to fetter his ideal thoughts with classic chains. His *Concertos* and *Sonatas* are beautiful indeed, but we may discern in them more effort than inspiration. His creative genius was imperious, fantastic and impulsive. His beauties were only manifested fully in entire freedom. We believe he offered violence to the character of his genius whenever he sought to subject it to rules, to classifications, to regulations not his own, and which he could not force into harmony with the exactions of his own mind. He was one of those original beings, whose graces are only fully displayed when they have cut themselves adrift from all bondage, and float on at their own wild will, swayed only by the ever undulating impulses of their own mobile natures.

He was, perhaps, induced to desire this double success through the example of his friend, Mickiewicz, who, having been the first to gift his country with romantic poetry, forming a school in Slavic literature by the publication of his *Dziady,* and his romantic Ballads, as early as 1818, proved afterwards, by the publication at his *Grazyna* and *Wallenrod,* that he could triumph over the difficulties that classic restrictions oppose to inspiration, and that, when holding the classic lyre of the ancient poets, he was still master. In making analogous attempts, we do not think Chopin has been equally successful. He could not retain, within the square of an angular and rigid mould, that floating and indeterminate contour which so fascinates us in his graceful conceptions. He could not introduce in its unyielding lines that shadowy and sketchy indecision, which, disguising the skeleton, the whole frame-work of form, drapes it in the mist of floating vapors, such as surround the white-bosomed maids of Ossian, when they permit mortals to catch some vague, yet lovely outline, from their home in the changing, drifting, blinding clouds.

Some of these efforts, however, are resplendent with a rare dignity of style; and passages of exceeding interest, of surprising grandeur, may be found among them. As an example of this, we cite the *Adagio* of the Second *Concerto*, for which he evinced a decided preference, and which he liked to repeat frequently. The accessory designs are in his best manner, while the principal phrase is of an admirable breadth. It alternates with a Recitative, which assumes a minor key, and which seems to be its Antistrophe. The whole of this piece is of a perfection almost ideal; its expression, now radiant with light, now full of tender pathos. It seems as if one had chosen a happy vale of Tempé, a magnificent landscape flooded with summer glow and lustre, as a background for the rehearsal of some dire scene of mortal anguish. A bitter and irreparable regret seizes the wildly-throbbing human heart, even in the midst of the incomparable splendor of external nature. This contrast is sustained by a fusion of tones, a softening of gloomy hues, which prevent the intrusion of aught rude or brusque that might awaken a dissonance in the touching impression produced, which, while saddening joy, soothes and softens the bitterness of sorrow.

It would be impossible to pass in silence the *Funeral March* inserted in the first Sonata, which was arranged for the orchestra, and performed, for the first time, at his own obsequies. What other accents could have been found capable of expressing, with the same heart-breaking effect, the emotions, the tears, which should accompany to the last long sleep, one who had taught in a manner so sublime, how great losses should be mourned? We once heard it remarked by a native of his own country: "these pages could only have been written by a Pole." All that the funeral train of an entire nation weeping its own ruin and death can be imagined to feel of desolating woe, of majestic sorrow, wails in the musical ringing of this passing bell, mourns in the tolling of this solemn knell, as it accompanies the mighty escort on its way to the still city of the Dead. The intensity of mystic hope; the devout appeal to superhuman pity, to infinite mercy, to a dread justice, which numbers every cradle and watches every tomb; the exalted resignation which has wreathed so much grief with halos so luminous; the noble endurance of so many disasters with the inspired heroism of Christian martyrs who know not to despair;—resound in this melancholy chant, whose voice of supplication breaks the heart. All of most pure, of most holy, of most believing, of most hopeful in the hearts of children, women, and priests, resounds, quivers and trembles there with irresistible vibrations. We feel it is not the death of a single warrior we mourn, while other heroes live to avenge him, but that a whole generation of warriors has forever fallen, leaving the death song to be chanted but by wailing women, weeping children and helpless priests. Yet this Mélopée so funereal, so full of desolating woe, is of such penetrating sweetness, that we can scarcely deem it of this earth. These sounds, in which the wild passion of human anguish seems chilled by awe and softened by distance, impose a profound meditation, as if, chanted by angels, they floated already in the heavens: the cry of a nation's anguish mounting to the very throne of God! The appeal of human grief from the lyre of seraphs! Neither cries, nor hoarse groans, nor impious blasphemies, nor furious imprecations, trouble for a moment the sublime sorrow of the plaint: it breathes upon the ear like the rhythmed sighs of angels. The antique face of grief is entirely excluded. Nothing recalls the fury of Cassandra, the prostration of Priam, the frenzy of Hecuba, the despair of the Trojan captives. A sublime faith destroying in the survivors of this Christian Ilion the bitterness of anguish and the cowardice of despair, their sorrow is no longer marked by earthly weakness. Raising itself from the soil wet with blood and tears, it springs forward to implore God; and, having nothing more to hope from earth, it supplicates the Supreme Judge with prayers so poignant, that our hearts, in listening, break under the weight of an august compassion!

It would be a mistake to suppose that all the compositions of Chopin are deprived of the feelings which he has deemed best to suppress in this great work. Not so. Perhaps human nature is not capable of maintaining always this mood of energetic abnegation, of courageous submission. We meet with breathings of stifled rage, of suppressed anger, in many passages of his writings: and many of his *Studies*, as well as his *Scherzos*, depict a concentrated exasperation and despair, which are sometimes manifested in bitter irony, sometimes in intolerant hauteur. These dark apostrophes of his muse have attracted less attention, have been less fully understood, than his poems of more tender coloring. The personal character of Chopin had something to do with this general misconception. Kind, courteous, and affable, of tranquil and almost joyous manners, he would not suffer the secret convulsions which agitated him to be even suspected.

His character was indeed not easily understood. A thousand subtle shades, mingling, crossing, contradicting and disguising each other, rendered it almost undecipherable at a first view. As is usually the case with the Sclaves, it was difficult to read the recesses of his mind. With them, loyalty and candor, familiarity and the most captivating ease of manner, by no means imply confidence, or impulsive frankness. Like the twisted folds of a serpent rolled upon itself, their feelings are half hidden, half revealed. It requires a most attentive examination to follow the coiled linking of the glittering rings. It would be naïve to interpret literally their courtesy full of compliment, their assumed humility. The forms of this politeness, this modesty, have their solution in their manners, in which their ancient connection with the East may be strangely traced. Without having in the least degree acquired the taciturnity of the Mussulman, they have yet learned from it a distrustful reserve upon all subjects which touch upon the more delicate and personal chords of the heart. When they speak of themselves, we may almost always be certain that they keep some concealment in reserve, which assures them the advantage in intellect, or feeling. They suffer their interrogator to remain in ignorance of some circumstance, some mobile secret, through the unveiling of which they would be more admired, or less esteemed, and which they well know how to hide under the subtle smile of an almost imperceptible mockery. Delighting in the pleasure of mystification, from the

most spiritual or comic to the most bitter and melancholy, they
may perhaps find in this deceptive raillery an external formula
of disdain for the veiled expression of the superiority which they
internally claim, but which claim they veil with the caution and
astuteness natural to the oppressed.

The frail and sickly organization of Chopin, not permitting
him the energetic expression of his passions, he gave to his
friends only the gentle and affectionate phase of his nature. In
the busy, eager life of large cities, where no one has time to study
the destiny of another, where everyone is judged by his external
activity, very few think it worthwhile to attempt to penetrate the
enigma of individual character. Those who enjoyed familiar
intercourse with Chopin, could not be blind to the impatience
and ennui he experienced in being, upon the calm character of
his manners, so promptly believed. And may not the artist
revenge the man? As his health was too frail to permit him to give
vent to his impatience through the vehemence of his execution,
he sought to compensate himself by pouring this bitterness over
those pages which he loved to hear performed with a vigor*
which he could not himself always command: pages which are
indeed full of the impassioned feelings of a man suffering deeply
from wounds which he does not choose to avow. Thus around a
gaily flagged, yet sinking ship, float the fallen spars and scattered
fragments, torn by warring winds and surging waves from its
shattered sides!

Such emotions have been of so much the more importance in
the life of Chopin, because they have deeply influenced the character of his compositions. Among the pages published under
such influences, may be traced much analogous to the wire-
drawn subtleties of Jean Paul, who found it necessary, in order to
move hearts macerated by passion, blasés through suffering, to
make use of the surprises caused by natural and physical phe-
nomena; to evoke the sensations of luxurious terrors arising from
occurrences not to be foreseen in the natural order of things; to
awaken the morbid excitements of a dreamy brain. Step by step

------

*It was his delight to hear them executed by the great Liszt himself.
                                                        —*Translator*.

the tortured mind of Chopin arrived at a state of sickly irritability; his emotions increased to a feverish tremor, producing that involution, that tortuosity of thought, which mark his latest works. Almost suffocating under the oppression of repressed feelings, using art only to repeat and rehearse for himself his own internal tragedy, after having wearied emotion, he began to subtilize it. His melodies are actually tormented; a nervous and restless sensibility leads to an obstinate persistence in the handling and rehandling and a reiterated pursuit of the tortured *motifs,* which impress us as painfully as the sight of those physical or mental agonies which we know can find relief only in death. Chopin was a victim to a disease without hope, which growing more envenomed from year to year, took him, while yet young, from those who loved him, and laid him in his still grave. As in the fair form of some beautiful victim, the marks of the grasping claws of the fierce bird of prey which has destroyed it, may be found; so, in the productions of which we have just spoken, the traces of the bitter sufferings which devoured his heart, are painfully visible.

CHAPTER II.

IT must not be supposed that the tortured aberrations of
feeling to which we have just alluded, ever injure the harmonic tissue in the works of Chopin; on the contrary, they
only render it a more curious subject for analysis. Such eccen-
tricities rarely occur in his more generally known and admired
compositions. His *Polonaises*, which are less studied than they
merit, on account of the difficulties presented by their perfect
execution, are to be classed among his highest inspirations.
They never remind us of the mincing and affected *"Polonaises
à la Pompadour,"* which our orchestras have introduced into
ball-rooms, our virtuosi in concerts, or of those to be found in
our "Parlor Repertories," filled, as they invariably are, with
hackneyed collections of music, marked by insipidity and
mannerism.

His *Polonaises*, characterized by an energetic rhythm, galva-
nize and electrify the torpor of indifference. The most noble tra-
ditional feelings of ancient Poland are embodied in them. The
firm resolve and calm gravity of its men of other days, breathe
through these compositions. Generally of a martial character,
courage and daring are rendered with that simplicity of expression, said to be a distinctive trait of this warlike people. They
bring vividly before the imagination, the ancient Poles, as we find
them described in their chronicles; gifted with powerful organizations, subtle intellects, indomitable courage and earnest piety,
mingled with high-born courtesy and a gallantry which never
deserted them, whether on the eve of battle, during its exciting
course, in the triumph of victory, or amidst the gloom of defeat.
So inherent was this gallantry and chivalric courtesy in their

nature, that in spite of the restraint which their customs (resembling those of their neighbours and enemies, the infidels of
Stamboul) induced them to exercise upon their women, confining them in the limits of domestic life and always holding them
under legal wardship, they still manifest themselves in their
annals, in which they have glorified and immortalized queens
who were saints; vassals who became queens, beautiful subjects
for whose sake some periled, while others lost, crowns: a terrible
Sforza; an intriguing d'Arquien; and a coquettish Gonzaga.

The Poles of olden times united a manly firmness with this
peculiar chivalric devotion to the objects of their love. A characteristic example of this may be seen in the letters of Jean
Sobieski to his wife. They were dictated in face of the standards
of the Crescent, "numerous as the ears in a grain-field," tender
and devoted as is their character. Such traits caught a singular
and imposing hue from the grave deportment of these men, so
dignified that they might almost be accused of pomposity. It was
next to impossible that they should not contract a taste for this
stateliness, when we consider that they had almost always
before them the most exquisite type of gravity of manner in the
followers of Islam, whose qualities they appreciated and appro-
priated, even while engaged in repelling their invasions. Like
the infidel, they knew how to preface their acts by an intelligent
deliberation, so that the device of Prince Boleslas of Pomerania,
was always present to them: "First weigh it; then dare:" *Erst
wieg's: dann wag's!* Such deliberation imparted a kind of stately
pride to their movements, while it left them in possession of an
ease and freedom of spirit accessible to the lightest cares of tenderness, to the most trivial interests of the passing hour, to the
most transient feelings of the heart. As it made part of their code
of honor to make those who interfered with them, in their more
tender interests, pay dearly for it; so they knew how to beautify
life, and, better still, they knew how to love those who embellished it; to revere those who rendered it precious to them.

Their chivalric heroism was sanctioned by their grave and
haughty dignity; an intelligent and premeditated conviction
added the force of reason to the energy of impulsive virtue; thus

they have succeeded in winning the admiration of all ages, of all minds, even that of their most determined adversaries. They were characterized by qualities rarely found together, the description of which would appear almost paradoxical: reckless wisdom, daring prudence, and fanatic fatalism. The most marked and celebrated historic manifestation of these properties is to be found in the expedition of Sobieski when he saved Vienna, and gave a mortal blow to the Ottoman Empire, which was at last conquered in the long struggle, sustained on both sides with so much prowess and glory, with so much mutual deference between opponents as magnanimous in their truces as irreconcilable in their combats.

While listening to some of the *Polonaises* of Chopin, we can almost catch the firm, nay, the more than firm, the heavy, resolute tread of men bravely facing all the bitter injustice which the most cruel and relentless destiny can offer, with the manly pride of unblenching courage. The progress of the music suggests to our imagination such magnificent groups as were designed by Paul Veronese, robed in the rich costume of days long past: we see passing at intervals before us, brocades of gold, velvets, damasked satins, silvery soft and flexile sables, hanging sleeves gracefully thrown back upon the shoulders, embossed sabres, boots yellow as gold or red with trampled blood, sashes with long and undulating fringes, close chemisettes, rustling trains, stomachers embroidered with pearls, headdresses glittering with rubies or leafy with emeralds, light slippers rich with amber, gloves perfumed with the luxurious attar from the harems. From the faded background of times long passed these vivid groups start forth; gorgeous carpets from Persia lie at their feet, filigreed furniture from Constantinople stands around; all is marked by the sumptuous prodigality of the Magnates who drew, in ruby goblets embossed with medallions, wine from the fountains of Tokay, and shoed their fleet Arabian steeds with silver, who surmounted all their escutcheons with the same crown which the fate of an election might render a royal one, and which, causing them to despise all other titles, was alone worn as *insigne* of their glorious equality.

Those who have seen the Polonaise danced even as late as the beginning of the present century, declare that its style has changed so much, that it is now almost impossible to divine its primitive character. As very few national dances have succeeded in preserving their racy originality, we may imagine, when we take into consideration the changes which have occurred, to what a degree this has degenerated. The Polonaise is without rapid movements, without any true steps in the artistic sense of the word, intended rather for display than for the exhibition of seductive grace; so we may readily conceive it must lose all its haughty importance, its pompous self-sufficiency, when the dancers are deprived of the accessories necessary to enable them to animate its simple form by dignified, yet vivid gestures, by appropriate and expressive pantomime, and when the costume peculiarly fitted for it is no longer worn. It has indeed become decidedly monotonous, a mere circulating promenade, exciting but little interest. Unless we could see it danced by some of the old regime who still wear the ancient costume, or listen to their animated descriptions of it, we can form no conception of the numerous incidents, the scenic pantomime, which once rendered it so effective. By a rare exception this dance was designed to exhibit the men, to display manly beauty, to set off noble and dignified deportment, martial yet courtly bearing. "Martial yet courtly": do not these two epithets almost define the Polish character? In the original the very name of the dance is masculine; it is only in consequence of a misconception that it has been translated in other tongues into the feminine gender.

Those who have never seen the *Kontusz* worn, (it is a kind of Occidental kaftan, as it is the robe of the Orientals, modified to suit the customs of an active life, unfettered by the stagnant resignation taught by fatalism,) a sort of *Feredgi*, often trimmed with fur, forcing the wearer to make frequent movements susceptible of grace and coquetry, by which the flowing sleeves are thrown backward, can scarcely imagine the bearing, the slow bending, the quick rising, the finesse of the delicate pantomime displayed by the Ancients, as they defiled in a Polonaise, as though in a military parade, not suffering their fingers to remain idle, but sometimes occupying them in playing with the long moustache, sometimes with the handle of the sword. Both moustache and sword were essential parts of the costume, and

were indeed objects of vanity with all ages. Diamonds and sap-
phires frequently sparkled upon the arms, worn suspended from
belts of cashmere, or from sashes of silk embroidered with gold,
displaying to advantage forms always slightly corpulent; the
moustache often veiled, without quite hiding, some scar, far
more effective than the most brilliant array of jewels. The dress
of the men rivaled that of the women in the luxury of the material worn, in the value of the precious stones, and in the variety
of vivid colors. This love of adornment is also found among the
Hungarians,° as may be seen in their buttons made of jewels,
the rings forming a necessary part of their dress, the wrought
clasps for the neck, the aigrettes and plumes adorning the cap
made of velvet of some brilliant hue. To know how to take off,
to put on, to manœuvre the cap with all possible grace, consti-
tuted almost an art. During the progress of a Polonaise, this
became an object of especial remark, because the cavalier of the
leading pair, as commandant of the file, gave the mute word of
command, which was immediately obeyed and imitated by the
rest of the train.

The master of the house in which the ball was given, always
opened it himself by leading off in this dance. His partner was
selected neither for her beauty, nor youth; the most highly honored lady present was always chosen. This phalanx, by whose
evolutions every fête was commenced, was not formed only of
the young: it was composed of the most distinguished, as well as
of the most beautiful. A grand review, a dazzling exhibition of all
the distinction present, was offered as the highest pleasure of
the festival. After the host, came next in order the guests of the
greatest consideration, who, choosing their partners, some from
friendship, some from policy or from desire of advancement,
some from love,—followed closely his steps. His task was a far
more complicated one than it is at present. He was expected to
conduct the files under his guidance through a thousand capricious meanderings, through long suites of apartments lined by

---

°The Hungarian costume worn by Prince Nicholas Esterhazy at the coronation
of George the Fourth, is still remembered in England. It was valued at several
millions of florins.

guests, who were to take a later part in this brilliant cortege. They liked to be conducted through distant galleries, through the parterres of illuminated gardens, through the groves of shrubbery, where distant echoes of the music alone reached the ear, which, as if in revenge, greeted them with redoubled sound and blowing of trumpets upon their return to the principal saloon. As the spectators, ranged like rows of hedges along the route, were continually changing, and never ceased for a moment to observe all their movements, the dancers never forgot that dignity of bearing and address which won for them the admiration of women, and excited the jealousy of men. Vain and joyous, the host would have deemed himself wanting in courtesy to his guests, had he not evinced to them, which he did sometimes with a piquant naïvete, the pride he felt in seeing himself surrounded by persons so illustrious, and partisans so noble, all striving through the splendor of the attire chosen to visit him, to show their high sense of the honor in which they held him.

Guided by him in their first circuit, they were led through long windings, where unexpected turns, views, and openings had been arranged beforehand to cause surprise; where architectural deceptions, decorations and shifting scenes had been studiously adapted to increase the pleasure of the festival. If any monument or inscription, fitted for the occasion, lay upon the long line of route, from which some complimentary homage might be drawn to the "most valiant or the most beautiful," the honors were gracefully done by the host. The more unexpected the surprises arranged for these excursions, the more imagination evinced in their invention, the louder were the applauses from the younger part of the society, the more ardent the exclamations of delight; and silvery sounds of merry laughter greeted pleasantly the ears of the conductor-in-chief, who, having thus succeeded in achieving his reputation, became a privileged Corypheus, a leader *par excellence.* If he had already attained a certain age, he was greeted on his return from such circuits by frequent deputations of young ladies, who came, in the name of all present, to thank and congratulate him. Through their vivid descriptions, these pretty wanderers excited the curiosity of the guests, and increased the eagerness for the formation of the succeeding Polonaises among those who, though they did not make part of the procession, still watched its passage in motionless attention, as if gazing upon the flashing line of light of some brilliant meteor.

In this land of aristocratic democracy, the numerous dependents of the great seigniorial houses, (too poor, indeed, to take part in the fête, yet only excluded from it by their own volition, all, however noble, some even more noble than their lords,) being all present, it was considered highly desirable to dazzle them; and this flowing chain of rainbow-hued and gorgeous light, like an immense serpent with its glittering rings, sometimes wreathed its linked folds, sometimes uncoiled its entire length, to display its brilliancy through the whole line of its undulating animated surface, in the most vivid scintillations; accompanying the shifting hues with the silvery sounds of chains of gold, ringing like muffled bells; with the rustling of the heavy sweep of gorgeous damasks and with the dragging of jewelled swords upon the floor. The murmuring sound of many voices announced the approach of this animated, varied, and glittering life-stream.

But the genius of hospitality, never deficient in high-born courtesy, and which, even while preserving the touching simplicity of primitive manners, inspired in Poland all the refinements of the most advanced state of civilization,—how could it be exiled from the details of a dance so eminently Polish? After the host had, by inaugurating the fête, rendered due homage to all who were present, any one of his guests had the right to claim his place with the lady whom he had honored by his choice. The new claimant, clapping his hands, to arrest for a moment the ever moving cortege, bowed before the partner of the host, begging her graciously to accept the change; while the host, from whom she had been taken, made the same appeal to the lady next in course. This example was followed by the whole train. Constantly changing partners, whenever a new cavalier claimed the honor of leading the one first chosen by the host, the ladies remained in the same succession during the whole course; while, on the contrary, as the gentlemen continually replaced each other, he who had commenced the dance, would, in its progress, become the last, if not indeed entirely excluded before its close.

Each cavalier who placed himself in turn at the head of the column, tried to surpass his predecessors in the novelty of the combinations of his opening, in the complications of the windings through which he led the expectant cortege; and this course, even when restricted to a single saloon, might be made remarkable by the designing of graceful arabesques, or the involved tracing of enigmatical ciphers. He made good his claim to the place he had solicited, and displayed his skill, by inventing close, complicated and inextricable figures; by describing them with so much certainty and accuracy, that the living ribbon, turned and twisted as it might be, was never broken in the loosing of its wreathed knots; and by so leading, that no confusion or graceless jostling should result from the complicated torsion. The succeeding couples, who had only to follow the figures already given, and thus continue the impulsion, were not permitted to drag themselves lazily and listlessly along the parquet. The step was rhythmic, cadenced, and undulating; the whole form swayed by graceful wavings and harmonious balancings. They were careful never to advance with too much haste, nor to replace each other as if driven on by some urgent necessity. On they glided, like swans descending a tranquil stream, their flexile forms swayed by the ebb and swell of unseen and gentle waves. Sometimes, the gentleman offered the right, sometimes, the left hand to his partner; touching only the points of her fingers, or clasping the slight hand within his own, he passed now to her right, now to her left, without yielding the snowy treasure. These complicated movements, being instantaneously imitated by every pair, ran, like an electric shiver, through the whole length of this gigantic serpent. Although apparently occupied and absorbed by these multiplied manœuvres, the cavalier yet found time to bend to his lady and whisper sweet flatteries in her ear, if she were young; if young no longer, to repose confidence, to urge requests, or to repeat to her the news of the hour. Then, haughtily raising himself, he would make the metal of his arms ring, caress his thick moustache, giving to all his features an expression so vivid, that the lady was forced to respond by the animation of her own countenance.

Thus, it was no hackneyed and senseless promenade which they executed; it was, rather, a parade in which the whole splendor of the society was exhibited, gratified with its own admiration, conscious of its own elegance, brilliancy, nobility and courtesy. It was a constant display of its lustre, its glory, its renown. Men grown gray in camps, or in the strife of courtly eloquence; generals more often seen in the cuirass than in the robes of peace; prelates and persons high in the Church; dignitaries of State aged senators; warlike palatines; ambitious castellans;—were the partners who were expected, welcomed, disputed and sought for, by the youngest, gayest, and most brilliant women present. Honor and glory rendered ages equal, and caused years to be forgotten in this dance; nay, more, they gave an advantage even over love. It was while listening to the animated descriptions of the almost forgotten evolutions and dignified capabilities of this truly national dance, from the lips of those who would never abandon the ancient *Zupan* and *Kontusz,* and who still wore their hair closely cut round their temples, as it had been worn by their ancestors, that we first fully understood in what a high degree this haughty nation possessed the innate instinct of its own exhibition, and how entirely it had succeeded, through its natural grace and genius, in poetizing its love of ostentation by draping it in the charms of noble emotions, and wrapping round it the glittering robes of martial glory.

When we visited the country of Chopin, whose memory always accompanied us like a faithful guide who constantly keeps our interest excited, we were fortunate enough to meet with some of the peculiar characters, daily growing more rare, because European civilization, even where it does not modify the basis of character, effaces asperities, and moulds exterior forms. We there encountered some of those men gifted with superior intellect, cultivated and strongly developed by a life of incessant action, yet whose horizon does not extend beyond the limits of their own country, their own society, their own traditions. During our intercourse, facilitated by an interpreter, with these men of past days, we were able to study them and to understand the secret of their greatness. It was really curious to observe the inimitable originality caused by the utter exclusiveness of the view taken by them. This limited cultivation, while it greatly diminishes the value of their ideas upon many subjects, at the same time gifts the mind with a peculiar force, almost resembling the keen scent and the acute perceptions of the savage, for all the things near and dear to it. Only from a mind of this peculiar training, marked by a concentrative energy that nothing can distract from its course, everything beyond the circle of its own nationality remaining alien to it, can we hope to obtain an exact picture of the past; for it alone, like a faithful mirror, reflects it in its primal coloring, preserves its proper lights and shades, and gives it with its varied and picturesque accompaniments. From such minds alone can we obtain, with the ritual of customs which are rapidly becoming extinct, the spirit from which they emanated. Chopin was born too late, and left the domestic hearth too early, to be himself in possession of this spirit; but he had known many examples of it, and, through the memories which surrounded his childhood, even more fully than through the literature and history of his country, he found by induction the secrets of its ancient prestige, which he evoked from the dim and dark land of forgetfulness, and, through the magic of his poetic art, endowed with immortal youth. Poets are better comprehended and appreciated by those who have made themselves familiar with the countries which inspired their songs. Pindar is more fully understood by those who have seen the Parthenon bathed in the radiance of its limpid atmosphere; Ossian, by those familiar with the mountains of Scotland, with their heavy veils and long wreaths of mist. The feelings which inspired the creations of Chopin can only be fully appreciated by those who have visited his country. They must have seen the giant shadows of past centuries gradually increasing, and veiling the ground as the gloomy night of despair rolled on; they must have felt the electric and mystic influence of that strange "phantom of glory" forever haunting martyred Poland. Even in the gayest hours of festival, it appalls and saddens all hearts. Whenever a tale of past renown, a commemoration of slaughtered heroes is given, an allusion to national prowess is made, its resurrection from the grave is instantaneous; it takes its place in the banquet-hall, spreading an electric terror mingled with intense admiration; a shudder, wild and mystic as that which seizes upon the peasants of Ukraine, when the "Beautiful Virgin," white as Death, with her girdle of crimson, is suddenly seen gliding through their tranquil village, while her shadowy

hand marks with blood the door of each cottage doomed to
destruction.

During many centuries, the civilization of Poland was entirely peculiar and aboriginal; it did not resemble that of any other
country; and, indeed, it seems destined to remain forever
unique in its kind. As different from the German feudalism
which neighboured it upon the West, as from the conquering
spirit of the Turks which disquieted it on the East, it resembled
Europe in its chivalric Christianity, in its eagerness to attack the
infidel, even while receiving instruction in sagacious policy, in
military tactics, and sententious reasoning, from the masters of
Byzantium. By the assumption, at the same time, of the heroic
qualities of Mussulman fanaticism and the sublime virtues of
Christian sanctity and humility,° it mingled the most heterogeneous elements, and thus planted in its very bosom the seeds
of ruin and decay.

The general culture of Latin letters, the knowledge of and
love for Italian and French literature gave a lustre and classical
polish to the startling contrasts we have attempted to describe.
Such a civilization must necessarily impress all its manifestations
with its own seal. As was natural for a nation always engaged in
war, forced to reserve its deeds of prowess and valor for its enemies upon the field of battle, it was not famed for the romances
of knight-errantry, for tournaments or jousts; it replaced the
excitement and splendor of the mimic war by characteristic
fetes, in which the gorgeousness of personal display formed the
principal feature.

There is certainly nothing new in the assertion, that national
character is, in some degree, revealed by national dances. We
believe, however, there are none in which the creative impulses

---

°It is well known with how many glorious names Poland has enriched the
martyrology of the Church. In memorial of the countless martyrs it had
offered, the Roman Church granted to the order of Trinitarians, or
Redemptorist Brothers, whose duty it was to redeem from slavery the
Christians who had fallen into the hands of the Infidels, the distinction, only
granted to this nation, of wearing a crimson belt. These victims to benevo-
lence were generally from the establishments near the frontiers, such as those
of Kamieniec-Podolski.

can be so readily deciphered, or the ensemble traced with so much simplicity, as in the Polonaise. In consequence of the varied episodes which each individual was expected to insert in the general frame, the national intuitions were revealed with the greatest diversity. When these distinctive marks disappeared, when the original flame no longer burned, when no one invented scenes for the intermediary pauses, when to accomplish mechanically the obligatory circuit of a saloon, was all that was requisite, nothing but the skeleton of departed glory remained.

We would certainly have hesitated to speak of the Polonaise, after the exquisite verses which Mickiewicz has consecrated to it, and the admirable description which he has given of it in the last Canto of the *Pan Tadeusz*, but that this description is to be found only in a work not yet translated, and, consequently, only known to the compatriots of the Poet.° It would have been presumptuous, even under another form, to have ventured upon a subject already sketched and colored by such a hand, in his romantic Epic, in which beauties of the highest order are set in such a scene as Ruysdäel loved to paint; where a ray of sunshine, thrown through heavy storm-clouds, falls upon one of those strange trees never wanting in his pictures, a birch shattered by lightning, while its snowy bark is deeply stained, as if dyed in the blood flowing from its fresh and gaping wounds. The scenes of *Pan Tadeusz* are laid at the beginning of the present century, when many still lived who retained the profound feeling and grave deportment of the ancient Poles, mingled with those who were even then under the sway of the graceful or giddying passions of modern origin. These striking and contrasting types existing together at that period, are now rapidly disappearing before that universal conventionalism which is at present seizing and moulding the higher classes in all cities and in all countries. Without doubt, Chopin frequently drew fresh inspiration from this noble poem, whose scenes so forcibly depict the emotions he best loved to reproduce.

The primitive music of the Polonaise, of which we have no

°It has been translated into German.—*T.*

example of greater age than a century, possesses but little value for art. Those Polonaises which do not bear the names of their authors, but are frequently marked with the name of some hero, thus indicating their date, are generally grave and sweet. The *Polonaise* styled *"de Kosciuszko,"* is the most universally known, and is so closely linked with the memories of his epoch, that we have known ladies who could not hear it without breaking into sobs. The Princess F. L., who had been loved by Kosciuszko, in her last days, when age had enfeebled all her faculties, was only sensible to the chords of this piece, which her trembling hands could still find upon the key-board, though the dim and aged eye could no longer see the keys. Some contemporary Polonaises are of a character so sad, that they might almost be supposed to accompany a funeral train.

The *Polonaises* of Count Oginsky[*] which next appeared, soon attained great popularity through the introduction of an air of seductive languor into the melancholy strains. Full of gloom as they still are, they soothe by their delicious tenderness, by their naïve and mournful grace. The martial rhythm grows more feeble; the march of the stately train, no longer rustling in its pride of state, is hushed in reverential silence, in solemn thought, as if its course wound on through graves, whose sad swells extinguish smiles and humiliate pride. Love alone survives, as the mourners wander among the mounds of earth so freshly heaped that the grass has not yet grown upon them, repeating the sad refrain which the Bard of Erin caught from the wild breezes of the sea:

"Love born of sorrow, like sorrow is true!"

In the well known pages of Oginsky may be found the sighing of analogous thoughts: the very breath of love is sad, and only revealed through the melancholy lustre of eyes bathed in tears.

At a somewhat later stage, the graves and grassy mounds were all passed, they are seen only in the distance of the shadowy

---

[*]Among the Polonaises of Count Oginsky, the one in *F Major* has especially retained its celebrity. It was published with a vignette, representing the author in the act of blowing his brains out with a pistol. This was merely a romantic commentary, which was for a long time mistaken for a fact.

background. The living cannot always weep; life and animation again appear, mournful thoughts changed into soothing memories, return on the ear, sweet as distant echoes. The saddened train of the living no longer hush their breath as they glide on with noiseless precaution, as if not to disturb the sleep of those who have just departed, over whose graves the turf is not yet green; the imagination no longer evokes only the gloomy shadows of the past. In the *Polonaises* of Lipinski we hear the music of the pleasure-loving heart once more beating joyously, giddily, happily, as it had done before the days of disaster and defeat. The melodies breathe more and more the perfume of happy youth; love, young love, sighs around. Expanding into expressive songs of vague and dreamy character, they speak but to youthful hearts, cradling them in poetic fictions, in soft illusions. No longer destined to cadence the steps of the high and grave personages who ceased to bear their part in these dances,* they are addressed to romantic imaginations, dreaming rather of rapture than of renown. Meyseder advanced upon this descending path; his dances, full of lively coquetry, reflect only the magic charms of youth and beauty. His numerous imitations have inundated us with pieces of music, called *Polonaises*, but which have no characteristics to justify the name.

The pristine and vigorous brilliancy of the *Polonaise* was again suddenly given to it by a composer of true genius. Weber made of it a Dithyrambic, in which the glittering display of vanished magnificence again appeared in its ancient glory. He united all the resources of his art to ennoble the formula which had been so misrepresented and debased, to fill it with the spirit of the past; not seeking to recall the character of ancient music, he transported into music the characteristics of ancient Poland. Using the melody as a recital, he accentuated the rhythm, he colored his composition, through his modulations, with a profusion of hues not only suitable to his subject, but imperiously demanded by it. Life, warmth, and passion again circulated in his *Polonaises*, yet he did not deprive them of the haughty

---

*Bishops and Primates formerly assisted in these dances; at a later date the Church dignitaries took no part in them.

charm, the ceremonious and magisterial dignity, the natural yet elaborate majesty, which are essential parts of their character. The cadences are marked by chords, which fall upon the ear like the rattling of swords drawn from their scabbards. The soft, warm, effeminate pleadings of love give place to the murmuring of deep, full, bass voices, proceeding from manly breasts used to command; we may almost hear, in reply, the wild and distant neighings of the steeds of the desert, as they toss the long manes around their haughty heads, impatiently pawing the ground, with their lustrous eye beaming with intelligence and full of fire, while they bear with stately grace the trailing caparisons embroidered with turquoise and rubies, with which the Polish Seigneurs loved to adorn them.° How did Weber divine the Poland of other days? Had he indeed the power to call from the grave of the past, the scenes which we have just contemplated, that he was thus able to clothe them with life, to renew their earlier associations? Vain questions! Genius is always endowed with its own sacred intuitions! Poetry ever reveals to her chosen the secrets of her wild domain!

°Among the treasures of Prince Radziwill at Nieswirz were to be seen, in the days of former splendor, twelve sets of horse trappings, each of a different color, incrusted with precious stones. The twelve Apostles, life size, in massive silver, were also to be seen there. This luxury will cease to astonish us when we consider that the family of Radziwill was descended from the last Grand Pontiff of Lithuania, to whom, when he embraced Christianity, were given all the forests and plains which had before been consecrated to the worship of the heathen Deities; and that toward the close of the last century, the family still possessed eight hundred thousand serfs, although its riches had then considerably diminished. Among the collection of treasures of which we speak, was an exceedingly curious relic, which is still in existence. It is a picture of St. John the Baptist, surrounded by a Bannerol bearing the inscription: "In the name of the Lord, John, thou shalt be Conqueror." It was found by Jean Sobieski himself, after the victory which he had won, under the walls of Vienna, in the tent of the Vizier Kara Mustapha. It was presented after his death, by Marie d'Arquin, to a Prince Radziwill, with an inscription in her own hand- writing which indicates its origin, and the presentation which she makes of it. The autograph, with the royal seal, is on the reverse side of the canvas.

All the poetry contained in the Polonaises had, like a rich sap, been so fully expressed from them by the genius of Weber, they had been handled with a mastery so absolute, that it was, indeed, a dangerous and difficult thing to attempt them, with the slightest hope of producing the same effect. He has, however, been surpassed in this species of composition by Chopin, not only in the number and variety of works in this style, but also in the more touching character of the handling, and the new and varied processes of harmony. Both in construction and spirit, Chopin's *Polonaise* in *A*, with the one in *A flat Major*, resembles very much the one of Weber's in E Major. In others he relinquished this broad style: Shall we say always with a more decided success? In such a question, decision were a thorny thing. Who shall restrict the rights of a poet over the various phases of his subject? Even in the midst of joy, may he not be permitted to be gloomy and oppressed? After having chanted the splendor of glory, may he not sing of grief? After having rejoiced with the victorious, may he not mourn with the vanquished? We may, without any fear of contradiction, assert, that it is not one of the least merits of Chopin, that he has, consecutively, embraced *all* the phases of which the theme is susceptible, that he has succeeded in eliciting from it all its brilliancy, in awakening from it all its sadness. The variety of the moods of feeling to which he was himself subject, aided him in the reproduction and comprehension of such a multiplicity of views. It would be impossible to follow the varied transformations occurring in these compositions, with their pervading melancholy, without admiring the fecundity of his creative force, even when not fully sustained by the higher powers of his inspiration. He did not always confine himself to the consideration of the pictures presented to him by his imagination and memory, taken en masse, or as a united whole. More than once, while contemplating the brilliant groups and throngs flowing on before him, has he yielded to the strange charm of some isolated figure, arresting it in its course by the magic of his gaze, and, suffering the gay crowds to pass on, he has given himself up with delight to the divination of its mystic revelations, while he continued to weave his incantations and spells only for the entranced Sibyl of his song.

His *Grand Polonaise* in *F sharp Minor*, must be ranked

among his most energetic compositions. He has inserted in it a *Mazourka*. Had he not frightened the frivolous world of fashionable life, by the gloomy grotesqueness with which he introduced it in an incantation so fantastic, this mode might have become an ingenious caprice for the ball-room. It is a most original production, exciting us like the recital of some broken dream, made, after a night of restlessness, by the first dull, gray, cold, leaden rays of a winter's sunrise. It is a dream-poem, in which the impressions and objects succeed each other with startling incoherency and with the wildest transitions, reminding us of what Byron says in his *"Dream"*:

> " . . . Dreams in their development have breath,
> And tears, and tortures, and the touch of joy;
> They leave a weight upon our waking thoughts,
> º　　　º　　　º　　　º　　　º　　　º　　　º
> And look like heralds of Eternity."

The principal motive is a weird air, dark as the lurid hour which precedes a hurricane, in which we catch the fierce exclamations of exasperation, mingled with a bold defiance, recklessly hurled at the stormy elements. The prolonged return of a tonic, at the commencement of each measure, reminds us of the repeated roar of artillery—as if we caught the sounds from some dread battle waging in the distance. After the termination of this note, a series of the most unusual chords are unrolled through measure after measure. We know nothing analogous, to the striking effect produced by this, in the compositions of the greatest masters. This passage is suddenly interrupted by a *Scène Champêtre*, a *Mazourka* in the style of an Idyl, full of the perfume of lavender and sweet marjoram; but which, far from effacing the memory of the profound sorrow which had before been awakened, only augments, by its ironical and bitter contrast, our emotions of pain to such a degree, that we feel almost solaced when the first phrase returns; and, free from the disturbing contradiction of a naïve, simple, and inglorious happiness, we may again sympathize with the noble and imposing woe of a high, yet fatal struggle. This improvisation terminates like a dream, without other conclusion than a convulsive shudder;

leaving the soul under the strangest, the wildest, the most subduing impressions.

The *"Polonaise-Fantaisie"* is to be classed among the works which belong to the latest period of Chopin's compositions, which are all more or less marked by a feverish and restless anxiety. No bold and brilliant pictures are to be found in it; the loud tramp of a cavalry accustomed to victory is no longer heard; no more resound the heroic chants muffled by no visions of defeat—the bold tones suited to the audacity of those who were always victorious. A deep melancholy—ever broken by startled movements, by sudden alarms, by disturbed rest, by stifled sighs—reigns throughout. We are surrounded by such scenes and feelings as might arise among those who had been surprised and encompassed on all sides by an ambuscade, the vast sweep of whose horizon reveals not a single ground for hope, and whose despair had giddied the brain, like a draught of that wine of Cyprus which gives a more instinctive rapidity to all our gestures, a keener point to all our words, a more subtle flame to all our emotions, and excites the mind to a pitch of irritability approaching insanity.

Such pictures possess but little real value for art. Like all descriptions of moments of extremity, of agonies, of death rattles, of contractions of the muscles where all elasticity is lost, where the nerves, ceasing to be the organs of the human will, reduce man to a passive victim of despair; they only serve to torture the soul. Deplorable visions, which the artist should admit with extreme circumspection within the graceful circle of his charmed realm!

CHAPTER III.

IN all that regards expression, the *Mazourkas* of Chopin differ
greatly from his *Polonaises*. Indeed they are entirely unlike in
character. The bold and vigorous coloring of the Polonaises
gives place to the most delicate, tender, and evanescent shades
in the Mazourkas. A nation, considered as a whole, in its united,
characteristic, and single impetus, is no longer placed before us;
the character and impressions now become purely personal,
always individualized and divided. No longer is the feminine
and effeminate element driven back into shadowy recesses. On
the contrary, it is brought out in the boldest relief, nay, it is
brought into such prominent importance that all else disap-
pears, or, at most, serves only as its accompaniment. The days
are now past when to say that a woman was charming, they
called her *grateful (wdzieczna)*; the very word charm being
derived from *wdzieki: gratitude.* Woman no longer appears as a
protégée, but as a queen; she no longer forms only the better
part of life, she now entirely fills it. Man is still ardent, proud,
and presumptuous, but he yields himself up to a delirium of
pleasure. This very pleasure is, however, always stamped with
melancholy. Both the music of the national airs, and the words,
which are almost always joined with them, express mingled
emotions of pain and joy. This strange but attractive contrast
was caused by the necessity of *"consoling misery" (cieszyc bide),*
which necessity induced them to seek the magical distraction of
the graceful Mazourka, with its transient delusions. The words
which were sung to these melodies, gave them a capability of
linking themselves with the sacred associations of memory, in a
far higher degree than is usual with ordinary dance-music. They
were sung and re-sung a thousand times in the days of buoyant

youth, by fresh and sonorous voices, in the hours of solitude, or in those of happy idleness. Linking the most varying associations with the melody, they were again and again carelessly hummed when traveling through forests, or ploughing the deep in ships; perhaps they were listlessly upon the lips when some startling emotion has suddenly surprised the singer; when an unexpected meeting, a long-desired grouping, an unhoped-for word, has thrown an undying light upon the heart, consecrating hours destined to live forever, and ever to shine on in the memory, even through the most distant and gloomy recesses of the constantly darkening future.

Such inspirations were used by Chopin in the most happy manner, and greatly enriched with the treasures of his handling and style. Cutting these diamonds so as to present a thousand facets, he brought all their latent fire to light, and re-uniting even their glittering dust, he mounted them in gorgeous caskets. Indeed what settings could he have chosen better adapted to enhance the value of his early recollections, or which would have given him more efficient aid in creating poems, in arranging scenes, in depicting episodes, in producing romances? Such associations and national memories are indebted to him for a reign far more extensive than the land which gave them birth. Placing them among those idealized types which art has touched and consecrated with her resplendent lustre, he has gifted them with immortality.

In order fully to understand how perfectly this setting suited the varying emotions which Chopin had succeeded in displaying in all the magic of their rainbow hues, we must have seen the Mazourka danced in Poland, because it is only there that it is possible to catch the haughty, yet tender and alluring, character of this dance. The cavalier, always chosen by the lady, seizes her as a conquest of which he is proud, striving to exhibit her loveliness to the admiration of his rivals, before he whirls her off in an entrancing and ardent embrace, through the tenderness of which the defiant expression of the victor still gleams, mingling with the blushing yet gratified vanity of the prize, whose beauty forms the glory of his triumph. There are few more delightful scenes than a ball in Poland. After the Mazourka has com-

menced, the attention, in place of being distracted by a multitude of people jostling against each other without grace or
order, is fascinated by one couple of equal beauty, darting forward, like twin stars, in free and unimpeded space. As if in the
pride of defiance, the cavalier accentuates his steps, quits his
partner for a moment, as if to contemplate her with renewed
delight, rejoins her with passionate eagerness, or whirls himself
rapidly round, as though overcome with the sudden joy and
yielding to the delicious giddiness of rapture. Sometimes, two
couples start at the same moment, after which a change of partners may occur between them; or a third cavalier may present
himself, and, clapping his hands, claim one of the ladies as his
partner. The queens of the festival are in turn claimed by the
most brilliant gentlemen present, courting the honor of leading
them through the mazes of the dance.

While in the Waltz and Galop, the dancers are isolated, and
only confused tableaux are offered to the bystanders; while the
Quadrille is only a kind of pass at arms made with foils, where
attack and defence proceed with equal indifference, where the
most nonchalant display of grace is answered with the same
nonchalance; while the vivacity of the Polka, charming, we con-
fess, may easily become equivocal; while Fandangos, Tarantulas
and Minuets, are merely little love-dramas, only interesting to
those who execute them, in which the cavalier has nothing to do
but to display his partner, and the spectators have no share but
to follow, tediously enough, coquetries whose obligatory movements are not addressed to them;—in the Mazourka, on the
contrary, they have also their part, and the rôle of the cavalier
yields neither in grace nor importance to that of his fair partner.

The long intervals which separate the successive appearance
of the pairs being reserved for conversation among the dancers,
when their turn comes again, the scene passes no longer only
among themselves, but extends from them to the spectators. It
is to them that the cavalier exhibits the vanity he feels in having
been able to win the preference of the lady who has selected
him; it is in their presence she has deigned to show him this
honor; she strives to please them, because the triumph of
charming them is reflected upon her partner, and their applause
may be made a part of the most flattering and insinuating

coquetry. Indeed, at the close of the dance, she seems to make him a formal offering of their suffrages in her favor. She bounds rapidly towards him and rests upon his arm,—a movement susceptible of a thousand varying shades which feminine tact and subtle feeling well know how to modify, ringing every change, from the most impassioned and impulsive warmth of manner to an air of the most complete "abandon."

What varied movements succeed each other in the course round the ball-room! Commencing at first with a kind of timid hesitation, the lady sways about like a bird about to take flight; gliding for some time on one foot only, like a skater, she skims the ice of the polished floor; then, running forward like a sportive child, she suddenly takes wing. Raising her veiling eyelids, with head erect, with swelling bosom and elastic bounds, she cleaves the air as the light bark cleaves the waves, and, like an agile woodnymph, seems to sport with space. Again she recommences her timid graceful gliding, looks round among the spectators, sends sighs and words to the most highly favored, then extending her white arms to the partner who comes to rejoin her, again begins her vigorous steps which transport her with magical rapidity from one end to the other of the ballroom. She glides, she runs, she flies; emotion colors her cheek, brightens her eye; fatigue bends her flexile form, retards her winged feet, until, panting and exhausted, she softly sinks and reclines in the arms of her partner, who, seizing her with vigorous arm, raises her a moment in the air, before finishing with her the last intoxicating round.

In this triumphal course, in which may be seen a thousand Atalantas as beautiful as the dreams of Ovid, many changes occur in the figures. The couples, in the first chain, commence by giving each other the hand; then forming themselves into a circle, whose rapid rotation dazzles the eye, they wreathe a living crown, in which each lady is the only flower of its own kind, while the glowing and varied colors are heightened by the uniform costume of the men, the effect resembling that of the dark-green foliage with which nature relieves her glowing buds and fragrant bloom. They all then dart forward together with a sparkling animation, a jealous emulation, defiling before the spectators as in a review—an enumeration of which would scarcely yield in interest to those given us, by Homer and Tasso, of the armies about to range themselves in the front of battle! At the close of an hour or two, the same circle again forms to end the dance; and on those days when amusement and pleasure fill all with an excited gayety, sparkling and glittering through those impressible temperaments like an aurora in a midnight sky, a general promenade is recommenced, and in its accelerated movements, we cannot detect the least symptom of fatigue among all these delicate yet enduring women; as if their light limbs possessed the flexible tenacity and elasticity of steel!

As if by intuition, all the Polish women possess the magical science of this dance. Even the least richly gifted among them know how to draw from it new charms. If the graceful ease and noble dignity of those conscious of their own power are full of attraction in it, timidity and modesty are equally full of interest. This is so because of all modern dances, it breathes most of pure love. As the dancers are always conscious that the gaze of the spectators is fastened upon them, addressing themselves constantly to them, there reigns in its very essence a mixture of innate tenderness and mutual vanity, as full of delicacy and propriety as of allurement.

The latent and unknown poetry, which was only indicated in the original Polish Mazourkas, was divined, developed, and brought to light, by Chopin. Preserving their rhythm, he ennobled their melody, enlarged their proportions; and—in order to paint more fully in these productions, which he loved to hear us call "pictures from the easel," the innumerable and widely-differing emotions which agitate the heart during the progress of this dance, above all, in the long intervals in which the cavalier has a right to retain his place at the side of the lady, whom he never leaves—he wrought into their tissues harmonic lights and shadows, as new in themselves as were the subjects to which he adapted them.

Coquetries, vanities, fantasies, inclinations, elegies, vague emotions, passions, conquests, struggles upon which the safety or favor of others depends, all—all, meet in this dance. How difficult it is to form a complete idea of the infinite gradations of passion—sometimes pausing, sometimes progressing, sometimes suing, sometimes ruling! In the country where the Mazourka

reigns from the palace to the cottage, these gradations are pursued, for a longer or shorter time, with as much ardor and
enthusiasm as malicious trifling. The good qualities and faults of
men are distributed among the Poles in a manner so fantastic,
that, although the essentials of character may remain nearly the
same in all, they vary and shade into each other in a manner so
extraordinary, that it becomes almost impossible to recognize or
distinguish them. In natures so capriciously amalgamated, a
wonderful diversity occurs, adding to the investigations of
curiosity, a spur unknown in other lands; making of every new
relation a stimulating study, and lending unwonted interest to
the lightest incident. Nothing is here indifferent, nothing
unheeded, nothing hackneyed! Striking contrasts are constantly
occurring among these natures so mobile and susceptible,
endowed with subtle, keen and vivid intellects, with acute
sensibilities increased by suffering and misfortune; contrasts
throwing lurid light upon hearts, like the blaze of a conflagration
illumining and revealing the gloom of midnight. Here chance
may bring together those who but a few hours before were
strangers to each other. The ordeal of a moment, a single word,
may separate hearts long united; sudden confidences are often
forced by necessity, and invincible suspicions frequently held in
secret. As a witty woman once remarked: "They often play a
comedy, to avoid a tragedy!" That which has never been uttered,
is yet incessantly divined and understood. Generalities are often
used to sharpen interrogation, while concealing its drift; the
most evasive replies are carefully listened to, like the ringing of
metal, as a test of the quality. Often, when in appearance plead-
ing for others, the suitor is urging his own cause; and the most
graceful flattery may be only the veil of disguised exactions.

But caution and attention become at last wearisome to
natures naturally expansive and candid, and a tiresome frivolity,
surprising enough before the secret of its reckless indifference
has been divined, mingles with the most spiritual refinement,
the most poetic sentiments, the most real causes for intense suffering, as if to mock and jeer at all reality. It is difficult to analyze or appreciate justly this frivolity, as it is sometimes real,
sometimes only assumed. It makes use of confusing replies and
strange resources to conceal the truth. It is sometimes justly,

sometimes wrongfully regarded as a kind of veil of motley, whose fantastic tissue needs only to be slightly torn to reveal more than one hidden or sleeping quality under the variegated folds of gossamer. It often follows from such causes, that eloquence becomes only a sort of grave badinage, sparkling with spangles like the play of fireworks, though the heart of the discourse may contain nothing earnest; while the lightest raillery, thrown out apparently at random, may perhaps be most sadly serious. Bitter and intense thought follows closely upon the steps of the most tempestuous gayety; nothing indeed remains absolutely superficial, though nothing is presented without an artificial polish. In the discussions constantly occurring in this country, where conversation is an art cultivated to the highest degree, and occupying much time, there are always those present, who, whether the topic discussed be grave or gay, can pass in a moment from smiles to tears, from joy to sorrow, leaving the keenest observer in doubt which is most real, so difficult is it to discern the fictitious from the true.

In such varying modes of thought, where ideas shift like quick sands upon the shores of the sea, they are rarely to be found again at the exact point where they were left. This fact is in itself sufficient to give interest to interviews otherwise insignificant. We have been taught this in Paris by some natives of Poland, who astonished the Parisians by their skill in "fencing in paradox"; an art in which every Pole is more or less skillful, as he has felt more or less interest or amusement in its cultivation. But the inimitable skill with which they are constantly able to alternate the garb of truth or fiction (like touchstones, more certain when least suspected, the one always concealed under the garb of the other), the force which expends an immense amount of intellect upon the most trivial occasions, as Gil Blas made use of as much intelligence to find the means of subsistence for a single day, as was required by the Spanish king to govern the whole of his domain; make at last an impression as painful upon us as the games in which the jugglers of India exhibit such wonderful skill, where sharp and deadly arms fly glittering through the air, which the least error, the least want of perfect mastery, would make the bright, swift messengers of certain death! Such skill is full of concealed anxiety, terror, and anguish! From the compli-

cation of circumstances, danger may lurk in the slightest inadvertence, in the least imprudence, in possible accidents, while
powerful assistance may suddenly spring from some obscure
and forgotten individual. A dramatic interest may instantaneously arise from interviews apparently the most trivial, giving
an unforeseen phase to every relation. A misty uncertainty hov-
ers round every meeting, through whose clouds it is difficult to
seize the contours, to fix the lines, to ascertain the present and
future influence, thus rendering intercourse vague and unintel-
ligible, filling it with an undefinable and hidden terror, yet, at
the same time, with an insinuating flattery. The strong currents
of genuine sympathy are always struggling to escape from the
weight of this external repression. The differing impulses of
vanity, love, and patriotism, in their threefold motives of action,
are forever hurtling against each other in all hearts, leading to
inextricable confusion of thought and feeling.

What mingling emotions are concentrated in the accidental
meetings of the Mazourka! It can surround, with its own
enchantment, the lightest emotion of the heart, while, through
its magic, the most reserved, transitory, and trivial rencounter
appeals to the imagination. Could it be otherwise in the presence of the women who give to this dance that inimitable grace
and suavity, for which, in less happy countries, they struggle in
vain? In very truth are not the Slavic women utterly incomparable? There are to be found among them those whose qualities
and virtues are so incontestable, so absolute, that they are
acknowledged by all ages, and by all countries. Such apparitions
are always and everywhere rare. The women of Poland are generally distinguished by an originality full of fire. Parisians in
their grace and culture, Eastern dancing girls in their languid
fire, they have perhaps preserved among them, handed down
from mother to daughter, the secret of the burning love potions
possessed in the seraglios. Their charms possess the strange spell
of Asiatic languor. With the flames of spiritual and intellectual
Houris in their lustrous eyes, we find the luxurious indolence of
the Sultana. Their manners caress without emboldening; the
grace of their languid movements is intoxicating; they allure by
a flexibility of form, which knows no restraint, save that of
perfect modesty, and which etiquette has never succeeded in

robbing of its willowy grace. They win upon us by those intonations of voice which touch the heart, and fill the eye with tender tears; by those sudden and graceful impulses which recall the spontaneity and beautiful timidity of the gazelle. Intelligent, cultivated, comprehending everything with rapidity, skillful in the use of all they have acquired; they are nevertheless as superstitious and fastidious as the lovely yet ignorant creatures adored by the Arabian prophet. Generous, devout, loving danger and loving love, from which they demand much, and to which they grant little; beyond everything they prize renown and glory. All heroism is dear to them. Perhaps there is no one among them who would think it possible to pay too dearly for a brilliant action; and yet, let us say it with reverence, many of them devote to obscurity their most holy sacrifices, their most sublime virtues. But however exemplary these quiet virtues of the home life may be, neither the miseries of private life, nor the secret sorrows which must prey upon souls too ardent not to be frequently wounded, can diminish the wonderful vivacity of their emotions, which they know how to communicate with the infallible rapidity and certainty of an electric spark. Discreet by nature and position, they manage the great weapon of dissimulation with incredible dexterity, skillfully reading the souls of others without revealing the secrets of their own. With that strange pride which disdains to exhibit characteristic or individual qualities, it is frequently the most noble virtues which are thus concealed. The internal contempt they feel for those who cannot divine them, gives them that superiority which enables them to reign so absolutely over those whom they have enthralled, flattered, subjugated, charmed; until the moment arrives when—loving with the whole force of their ardent souls, they are willing to brave and share the most bitter suffering, prison, exile, even death itself, with the object of their love! Ever faithful, ever consoling, ever tender, ever unchangeable in the intensity of their generous devotion! Irresistible beings, who in fascinating and charming, yet demand an earnest and devout esteem! In that precious incense of praise burned by M. de Balzac, "in honor of that daughter of a foreign soil," he has thus sketched the Polish woman in hues composed entirely of antitheses: "Angel through love, demon through fantasy; child through faith, sage through experience; man through the brain, woman through the heart; giant through hope, mother through sorrow; and poet through dreams."°

The homage inspired by the Polish women is always fervent. They all possess the poetic conception of an ideal, which gleams through their intercourse like an image constantly passing before a mirror, the comprehension and seizure of which they impose as a task. Despising the insipid and common pleasure of merely being able to please, they demand that the being whom they love shall be capable of exacting their esteem. This romantic temperament sometimes retains them long in hesitation between the world and the cloister. Indeed, there are few among them who at some moment of their lives have not seriously and bitterly thought of taking refuge within the walls of a convent.

Where such women reign as sovereigns, what feverish words, what hopes, what despair, what entrancing fascinations must occur in the mazes of the Mazourka; the Mazourka, whose every cadence vibrates in the ear of the Polish lady as the echo of a vanished passion, or the whisper of a tender declaration. Which among them has ever danced through a Mazourka, whose cheeks burned not more from the excitement of emotion than from mere physical fatigue? What unexpected and endearing ties have been formed in the long *tête-à-tête*, in the very midst of crowds, with the sounds of music, which generally recalled the name of some hero or some proud historical remembrance attached to the words, floating around, while thus the associations of love and heroism became forever attached to the words and melodies! What ardent vows have been exchanged; what wild and despairing farewells been breathed! How many brief attachments have been linked and as suddenly unlinked, between those who had never met before, who were never, never to meet again—and yet, to whom forgetfulness had become forever impossible! What hopeless love may have been revealed during the moments so rare upon this earth; when beauty is more highly esteemed than riches, a noble bearing of

---

°Dedication of *"Modeste Mignon."*

more consequence than rank! What dark destinies forever sev-
ered by the tyranny of rank and wealth may have been, in these
fleeting moments of meeting, again united, happy in the glitter of
passing triumph, reveling in concealed and unsuspected joy! What
interviews, commenced in indifference, prolonged in jest, interrupted with emotion, renewed with the secret consciousness of
mutual understanding, (in all that concerns subtle intuition
Slavic finesse and delicacy especially excel) have terminated in
the deepest attachments! What holy confidences have been
exchanged in the spirit of that generous frankness which circulates from unknown to unknown, when the noble are delivered
from the tyranny of forced conventionalisms! What words
deceitfully bland, what vows, what desires, what vague hopes
have been negligently thrown on the winds;—thrown as the
handkerchief of the fair dancer in the Mazourka . . . and which
the maladroit knows not how to pick up! . . .

We have before asserted that we must have known personally
the women of Poland, for the full and intuitive comprehension of
the feelings with which the *Mazourkas* of Chopin, as well as
many more of his compositions, are impregnated. A subtle love
vapor floats like an ambient fluid around them; we may trace
step by step in his *Preludes, Nocturnes Impromptus* and
Mazourkas, all the phases of which passion is capable. The
sportive hues of coquetry the insensible and gradual yielding of
inclination, the capricious festoons of fantasy; the sadness of sickly joys born dying, flowers of mourning like the black roses, the
very perfume of whose gloomy leaves is depressing, and whose
petals are so frail that the faintest sigh is sufficient to detach
them from the fragile stem; sudden flames without thought, like
the false shining of that decayed and dead wood which only glit-
ters in obscurity and crumbles at the touch; pleasures without
past and without future, snatched from accidental meetings; illusions, inexplicable excitements tempting to adventure, like the
sharp taste of half-ripened fruit which stimulates and pleases
even while it sets the teeth on edge; emotions without memory
and without hope; shadowy feelings whose chromatic tints are
interminable;—are all found in these works, endowed by genius
with the innate nobility, the beauty, the distinction, the surpassing elegance of those by whom they are experienced.

In the compositions just mentioned, as well as in most of his *Ballads, Waltzes* and *Etudes*, the rendering of some of the poetical subjects to which we have just alluded, may be found embalmed. These fugitive poems are so idealized, rendered so fragile and attenuated, that they scarcely seem to belong to human nature, but rather to a fairy world, unveiling the indiscreet confidences of Peris, of Titanias, of Ariels, of Queen Mabs, of the Genii of the air, of water, and of fire,—like ourselves, subject to bitter disappointments, to invincible disgusts.

Some of these compositions are as gay and fantastic as the wiles of an enamored, yet mischievous sylph; some are soft, playing in undulating light, like the hues of a salamander; some, full of the most profound discouragement, as if the sighs of souls in pain, who could find none to offer up the charitable prayers necessary for their deliverance, breathed through their notes. Sometimes a despair so inconsolable is stamped upon them, that we feel ourselves present at some Byronic tragedy, oppressed by the anguish of a Jacopo Foscari, unable to survive the agony of exile. In some we hear the shuddering spasms of suppressed sobs. Some of them, in which the black keys are exclusively taken, are acute and subtle, and remind us of the character of his own gaiety, lover of atticism as he was, subject only to the higher emotions, recoiling from all vulgar mirth, from coarse laughter, and from low enjoyments, as we do from those animals more abject than venomous, whose very sight causes the most nauseating repulsion in tender and sensitive natures.

An exceeding variety of subjects and impressions occur in the great number of his Mazourkas. Sometimes we catch the manly sounds of the rattling of spurs, but it is generally the almost imperceptible rustling of crape and gauze under the light breath of the dancers, or the clinking of chains of gold and diamonds, that maybe distinguished. Some of them seem to depict the defiant pleasure of the ball given on the eve of battle, tortured however by anxiety for, through the rhythm of the dance, we hear the sighs and despairing farewells of hearts forced to suppress their tears. Others reveal to us the discomfort and secret ennui of those guests at a fête, who find it in vain to expect that the gay sounds will muffle the sharp cries of anguished spirits. We sometimes catch the gasping breath of terror and stifled

fears; sometimes divine the dim presentiments of a love destined to perpetual struggle and doomed to survive all hope,
which, though devoured by jealousy and conscious that it can
never be the victor, still disdains to curse, and takes refuge in a
soul-subduing pity. In others we feel as if borne into the heart of
a whirlwind, a strange madness; in the midst of the mystic confusion, an abrupt melody passes and repasses, panting and palpitating, like the throbbing of a heart faint with longing, gasping
in despair, breaking in anguish, dying of hopeless, yet indignant
love. In some we hear the distant flourish of trumpets, like fading memories of glories past. In some of them, the rhythm is as
floating, as undetermined, as shadowy, as the feeling with which
two young lovers gaze upon the first star of evening, as yet alone
in the dim skies.

Upon one afternoon, when there were but three persons present, and Chopin had been playing for a long time, one of the most
distinguished women in Paris remarked, that she felt always more
and more filled with solemn meditation, such as might be awakened in presence of the grave-stones strewing those grounds in
Turkey, whose shady recesses and bright beds of flowers promise
only a gay garden to the startled traveller. She asked him what was
the cause of the involuntary, yet sad veneration which subdued her
heart while listening to these pieces, apparently presenting only
sweet and graceful subjects:—and by what name he called the
strange emotion inclosed in his compositions, like ashes of the
unknown dead in superbly sculptured urns of the purest
alabaster. . . . Conquered by the appealing tears which moistened
the beautiful eyes, with a candor rare indeed in this artist, so susceptible upon all that related to the secrets of the sacred relics
buried in the gorgeous shrines of his music, he replied: "that her
heart had not deceived her in the gloom which she felt stealing
upon her, for whatever might have been his transitory pleasures,
he had never been free from a feeling which might almost be said
to form the soil of his heart, and for which he could find no appropriate expression except in his own language, no other possessing
a term equivalent to the Polish word: *Żal!*" As if his ear thirsted for
the sound of this word, which expresses the whole range of emotions produced by an intense regret, through all the shades of feeling, from hatred to repentance, he repeated it again and again.

Żal! Strange substantive, embracing a strange diversity, a strange philosophy! Susceptible of different regimens, it includes all the tenderness, all the humility of a regret borne with resignation and without a murmur, while bowing before the fiat of necessity, the inscrutable decrees of Providence: but, changing its character, and assuming the regimen indirect as soon as it is addressed to man, it signifies excitement, agitation, rancor, revolt full of reproach, premeditated vengeance, menace never ceasing to threaten if retaliation should ever become possible, feeding itself meanwhile with a bitter, if sterile hatred.

Żal! In very truth, it colors the whole of Chopin's compositions: sometimes wrought through their elaborate tissue, like threads of dim silver; sometimes coloring them with more passionate hues. It may be found in his sweetest reveries; even in those which that Shakespearian genius, Berlioz, comprehending all extremes, has so well characterized as "divine coquetries"— coquetries only understood in semi-oriental countries; coquetries in which men are cradled by their mothers, with which they are tormented by their sisters, and enchanted by those they love; and which cause the coquetries of other women to appear insipid or coarse in their eyes; inducing them to exclaim, with an appearance of boasting, yet in which they are entirely justified by the truth: *Niema iak Polki!* "Nothing equals the Polish women!"° Through the secrets of these "divine coquetries" those adorable beings are formed, who are alone capable of fulfilling the impassioned ideals of poets who, like M. de Chateaubriand, in the feverish sleeplessness of their adolescence, create for themselves visions "of an Eve, innocent, yet fallen; ignorant of all, yet knowing all; mistress, yet virgin."† The only being which was ever found to resemble this dream, was a Polish girl of seventeen—"a mixture of the Odalisque and Valkyria . . . realization of the ancient sylph—new Flora—freed from the chain of the seasons"‡—and whom M. de Chateaubriand feared to meet

---

°The custom formerly in use of drinking, in her own shoe, the health of the woman they loved, is one of the most original traditions of the enthusiastic gallantry of the Poles.
†*Memoires d'Outre Tombe.* 1st vol. *Incantation.*
‡Idem. 3d vol. *Atala.*

again. "Divine coquetries" at once generous and avaricious; impressing the floating, wavy, rocking, undecided motion of a boat without rigging or oars upon the charmed and intoxicated heart!

Through his peculiar style of performance, Chopin imparted this constant rocking with the most fascinating effect; thus making the melody undulate to and fro, like a skiff driven on over the bosom of tossing waves. This manner of execution, which set a seal so peculiar upon his own style of playing, was at first indicated by the term *Tempo rubato*, affixed to his writings: a Tempo agitated, broken, interrupted, a movement flexible, yet at the same time abrupt and languishing, and vacillating as the flame under the fluctuating breath by which it is agitated. In his later productions we no longer find this mark. He was convinced that if the performer understood them, he would divine this rule of irregularity. All his compositions should be played with this accentuated and measured swaying and balancing. It is difficult for those who have not frequently heard him play to catch this secret of their proper execution. He seemed desirous of imparting this style to his numerous pupils, particularly those of his own country. His countrymen, or rather his countrywomen, seized it with the facility with which they understand everything relating to poetry or feeling; an innate, intuitive comprehension of his meaning aided them in following all the fluctuations of his depths of aerial and spiritual blue.

CHAPTER IV.

Chopin's Mode of Playing—Concerts—The Elite—Fading Bouquets and Immortal Crowns—Hospitality—Heine—Meyerbeer—Adolphe Nourrit—Eugène Delacroix—Niemcevicz—Mickiewicz—George Sand

AFTER having described the compositions palpitating with emotion in which genius struggles with grief, (grief, that terrible reality which Art must strive to reconcile with Heaven), confronting it sometimes as conqueror, sometimes as conquered; compositions in which all the memories of his youth, the affections of his heart, the mysteries of his desires, the secrets of his untold passions, are collected like tears in a lachrymatory; compositions in which, passing the limits of human sensations—too dull for his eager fancy, too obtuse for his keen perceptions—he makes incursions into the realms of Dryads, Oreads, and Oceanides;—we would naturally be expected to speak of his talent for execution. But this task we cannot assume. We cannot command the melancholy courage to exhume emotions linked with our fondest memories, our dearest personal recollections; we cannot force ourselves to make the mournful effort to color the gloomy shrouds, veiling the skill we once loved, with the brilliant hues they would exact at our hands. We feel our loss too bitterly to attempt such an analysis. And what result would it be possible to attain with all our efforts! We could not hope to convey to those who have never heard him, any just conception of that fascination so ineffably poetic, that charm subtle and penetrating as the delicate perfume of the vervain or the Ethiopian calla, which, shrinking and exclusive, refuses to diffuse its exquisite aroma in the noisome breath of crowds, whose heavy air can only retain the stronger odor of the tuberose, the incense of burning resin.

By the purity of its handling, by its relation with *La Fée aux miettes* and *Les Lutins d'Argail,* by its rencounters with the

45

Seraphins and *Dianes,* who murmur in his ear their most confi-
dential complaints, their most secret dreams, the style and the
manner of conception of Chopin remind us of Nedier. He knew
that he did not act upon the masses, that he could not warm the
multitude, which is like a sea of lead, and as heavy to set in
motion, and which, though its waves may be melted and rendered malleable by heat, requires the powerful arm of an
athletic Cyclops to manipulate, fuse, and pour into moulds,
where the dull metal, glowing and seething under the electric
fire, becomes thought and feeling under the new form into
which it has been forced. He knew he was only perfectly appreciated in those meetings, unfortunately too few, in which *all* his
hearers were prepared to follow him into those spheres which
the ancients imagined to be entered only through a gate of ivory,
to be surrounded by pilasters of diamond, and surmounted by a
dome arched with fawn-colored crystal, upon which played the
various dyes of the prism; spheres, like the Mexican opal, whose
kaleidoscopical foci are dimmed by olive-colored mists veiling
and unveiling the inner glories; spheres, in which all is magical
and supernatural, reminding us of the marvellous worlds of realized dreams. In such spheres Chopin delighted. He once
remarked to a friend, an artist who has since been frequently
heard: "I am not suited for concert giving; the public intimidate
me; their looks, only stimulated by curiosity, paralyze me; their
strange faces oppress me; their breath stifles me: but you—you
are destined for it, for when you do not gain your public, you
have the force to assault, to overwhelm, to control, to compel
them."

Conscious of how much was necessary for the comprehension
of his peculiar talent, he played but rarely in public. With the
exception of some concerts given at his début in 1831, in Vienna
and Munich, he gave no more, except in Paris, being indeed not
able to travel on account of his health, which was so precarious,
that during entire months, he would appear to be in an almost
dying state. During the only excursion which he made with a
hope that the mildness of a Southern climate would be more
conducive to his health, his condition was frequently so alarming, that more than once the hotel keepers demanded payment
for the bed and mattress he occupied, in order to have them

burned, deeming him already arrived at that stage of consumption in which it becomes so highly contagious.

We believe, however, if we may be permitted to say it, that his concerts were less fatiguing to his physical constitution, than to his artistic susceptibility. We think that his voluntary abnegation of popular applause veiled an internal wound. He was perfectly aware of his own superiority; perhaps it did not receive sufficient reverberation and echo from without to give him the tranquil assurance that he was perfectly appreciated. No doubt, in the absence of popular acclamation, he asked himself how far a chosen audience, through the enthusiasm of its applause, was able to replace the great public which he relinquished. Few understood him:—did those few indeed understand him aright? A gnawing feeling of discontent, of which he himself scarcely comprehended the cause, secretly undermined him. We have seen him almost shocked by eulogy. The praise to which he was justly entitled not reaching him *en masse*, he looked upon isolated commendation as almost wounding. That he felt himself not only slightly, but badly applauded, was sufficiently evident by the polished phrases with which, like troublesome dust, he shook such praises off, making it quite evident that he preferred to be left undisturbed in the enjoyment of his solitary feelings to injudicious commendation.

Too fine a connoisseur in raillery, too ingenious a satirist ever to expose himself to sarcasm, he never assumed the rôle of a "genius misunderstood." With a good grace and under an apparent satisfaction, he concealed so entirely the wound given to his just pride, that its very existence was scarcely suspected. But not without reason, might the gradually increasing rarity° of his concerts be attributed rather to the wish he felt to avoid occasions which did not bring him the tribute he merited, than to physical debility. Indeed, he put his strength to rude proofs in the many lessons which he always gave, and the many hours he spent at his own Piano.

It is to be regretted that the indubitable advantage for the

°Sometimes he passed years without giving a single concert. We believe the one given by him in Pleyel's room, in 1844, was after an interval of nearly ten years.

artist resulting from the cultivation of only a select audience, should be so sensibly diminished by the rare and cold expression of its sympathies. The *glacé* which covers the grace of the *élite*, as it does the fruit of their desserts; the imperturbable calm of their most earnest enthusiasm, could not be satisfactory to Chopin. The poet, torn from his solitary inspiration, can only find it again in the interest, more than attentive, vivid and animated of his audience. He can never hope to regain it in the cold looks of an Areopagus assembled to judge him. He must *feel* that he moves, that he agitates those who hear him, that his emotions find in them the responsive sympathies of the same intuitions, that he draws them on with him in his flight towards the infinite: as when the leader of a winged train gives the signal of departure, he is immediately followed by the whole flock in search of milder shores.

But had it been otherwise—had Chopin everywhere received the exalted homage and admiration he so well deserved; had he been heard, as so many others, by all nations and in all climates; had he obtained those brilliant ovations which make a Capitol everywhere, where the people salute merit or honor genius, had he been known and recognized by thousands in place of the hundreds who acknowledged him—we would not pause in this part of his career to enumerate such triumphs.

What are the dying bouquets of an hour to those whose brows claim the laurel of immortality? Ephemeral sympathies, transitory praises, are not to be mentioned in the presence of the august Dead, crowned with higher glories. The joys, the consolations, the soothing emotions which the creations of true art awaken in the weary, suffering, thirsty, or persevering and believing hearts to whom they are dedicated, are destined to be borne into far countries and distant years, by the sacred works of Chopin. Thus an unbroken bond will be established between elevated natures, enabling them to understand and appreciate each other, in whatever part of the earth or period of time they may live. Such natures are generally badly divined by their contemporaries when they have been silent, often misunderstood when they have spoken the most eloquently!

"There are different crowns," says Goethe, "there are some which may be readily gathered during a walk." Such crowns charm for the moment through their balmy freshness, but who would think of comparing them with those so laboriously gained by Chopin by constant and exemplary effort, by an earnest love of art, and by his own mournful experience of the emotions which he has so truthfully depicted?

As he sought not with a mean avidity those crowns so easily won, of which more than one among ourselves has the modesty to be proud; as he was a pure, generous, good and compassionate man, filled with a single sentiment, and that one of the most noble of feelings, the love of country; as he moved among us like a spirit consecrated by all that Poland possesses of poetry; let us approach his sacred grave with due reverence! Let us adorn it with no artificial wreaths! Let us cast upon it no trivial crowns! Let us nobly elevate our thoughts before this consecrated shroud! Let us learn from him to repulse all but the highest ambition, let us try to concentrate our labor upon efforts which will leave more lasting effects than the vain leading of the fashions of the passing hour. Let us renounce the corrupt spirit of the times in which we live, with all that is not worthy of art, all that will not endure, all that does not contain in itself some spark of that eternal and immaterial beauty, which it is the task of art to reveal and unveil as the condition of its own glory! Let us remember the ancient prayer of the Dorians whose simple formula is so full of pious poetry, asking only of their gods: "To give them the Good, in return for the Beautiful!" In place of laboring so constantly to attract auditors, and striving to please them at whatever sacrifice, let us rather aim, like Chopin, to leave a celestial and immortal echo of what we have felt, loved, and suffered! Let us learn, from his revered memory, to demand from ourselves works which will entitle us to some true rank in the sacred city of art! Let us not exact from the present without regard to the future, those light and vain wreaths which are scarcely woven before they are faded and forgotten! . . .

In place of such crowns, the most glorious palms which it is possible for an artist to receive during his lifetime, have been placed in the hands of Chopin by *illustrious equals*. An enthusiastic admiration was given him by a public still more limited than the musical aristocracy which frequented his concerts. This public was formed of the most distinguished names of men, who bowed before him as the kings of different empires bend before a monarch whom they have assembled to honor. Such men rendered to him, individually, due homage. How could it have been otherwise in France, where the hospitality, so truly national, discerns with such perfect taste the rank and claims of the guests?

The most eminent minds in Paris frequently met in Chopin's saloon. Not in reunions of fantastic periodicity, such as the dull imaginations of ceremonious and tiresome circles have arranged, and which they have never succeeded in realizing in accordance with their wishes, for enjoyment, ease, enthusiasm, animation, never come at an hour fixed upon beforehand. They can be commanded less by artists than by other men, for they are all more or less struck by some sacred malady whose paralyzing torpor they must shake off, whose benumbing pain they must forget, to be joyous and amused by those pyrotechnic fires which startle the bewildered guests, who see from time to time a Roman candle, a rose-colored Bengal light, a cascade whose waters are of fire, or a terrible, yet quite innocent dragon! Gayety and the strength necessary to be joyous, are, unfortunately things only accidentally to be encountered among poets and artists! It is true some of the more privileged among them have the happy gift of surmounting internal pain, so as to bear their burden always lightly, able to laugh with their companions over the toils of the way, or at least always able to preserve a gentle and calm serenity which, like a mute pledge of hope and consolation, animates, elevates, and encourages their associates, imparting to them, while they remain under the influence of this placid atmosphere, a freedom of spirit which appears so much the more vivid, the more strongly it contrasts with their habitual ennui, their abstraction, their natural gloom, their usual indifference.

Chopin did not belong to either of the above-mentioned classes; he possessed the innate grace of a Polish welcome, by which the host is not only bound to fulfill the common laws and duties of hospitality, but is obliged to relinquish all thought of himself, to devote all his powers to promote the enjoyment of his guests. It was a pleasant thing to visit him; his visitors were always charmed; he knew how to put them at once at ease, making them masters of every thing, and placing everything at their disposal. In doing the honors of his own cabin, even the simple laborer of Slavic race never departs from this munificence; more joyously eager in his welcome than the Arab in his tent, he compensates for the splendor which may be wanting in his reception by an adage which he never fails to repeat, and which is also repealed by the grand seignior after the most luxurious repasts served under gilded canopies: *Czym bohat, tym rad*—which is thus paraphrased for foreigners: "Deign graciously to pardon all that is unworthy of you, it is all my humble riches which I place at your feet." This formula° is still pronounced with a national grace and dignity by all masters of families who preserve the picturesque customs which distinguished the ancient manners of Poland.

Having thus described something of the habits of hospitality common in his country, the ease which presided over our reunions with Chopin will be readily understood. The flow of thought, the entire freedom from restraint, were of a character so pure that no insipidity or bitterness ever ensued, no ill humor was ever provoked. Though he avoided society, yet when his saloon was invaded, the kindness of his attention was delightful; without appearing to occupy himself with any one, he succeeded in finding for all that which was most agreeable; neglecting none, he extended to all the most graceful courtesy.

It was not without a struggle, without a repugnance slightly misanthropic, that Chopin could be induced to open his doors and piano, even to those whose friendship, as respectful as faithful, gave them a claim to urge such a request with eagerness. Without doubt more than one of us can still remember our first improvised evening with him, in spite of his refusal, when he lived at Chaussée d'Antin.

His apartment, invaded by surprise, was only lighted by some

°All the Polish formulas of courtesy retain the strong impress of the hyperbolical expressions of the Eastern languages. The titles of "very powerful and very enlightened seigniors" are still obligatory. The Poles, in conversation, constantly name each other Benefactor (*Dobrodzij*). The common salutation between men, and of men to women, is *Padam do Nog:* "I fall at your feet." The greeting of the people possesses a character of ancient solemnity and simplicity: *Sława Bohu:* "Glory to God."]

wax candles, grouped round one of Pleyel's pianos, which he
particularly liked for their slightly veiled, yet silvery sonorousness, and easy touch, permitting him to elicit tones which one
might think proceeded from one of those harmonicas of which
romantic Germany has preserved the monopoly, and which
were so ingeniously constructed by its ancient masters, by the
union of crystal and water.

As the corners of the room were left in obscurity, all idea of
limit was lost, so that there seemed no boundary save the darkness of space. Some tall piece of furniture, with its white cover,
would reveal itself in the dim light; an indistinct form, raising
itself like a spectre to listen to the sounds which had evoked it.
The light, concentrated round the piano and falling on the floor,
glided on like a spreading wave until it mingled with the broken
flashes from the fire, from which orange colored plumes rose
and fell, like fitful gnomes, attracted there by mystic incantations in their own tongue. A single portrait, that of a pianist, an
admiring and sympathetic friend, seemed invited to be the constant auditor of the ebb and flow of tones, which sighed,
moaned, murmured, broke and died upon the instrument near
which it always hung. By a strange accident, the polished surface
of the mirror only reflected so as to double it for our eyes, the
beautiful oval with silky curls which so many pencils have
copied, and which the engraver has just reproduced for all who
are charmed by works of such peculiar eloquence.

Several men, of brilliant renown, were grouped in the luminous zone immediately around the piano: Heine, the saddest of
humorists, listened with the interest of a fellow countryman to
the narrations made him by Chopin of the mysterious country
which haunted his ethereal fancy also, and of which he too had
explored the beautiful shores. At a glance, a word, a tone,
Chopin and Heine understood each other; the musician replied
to the questions murmured in his ear by the poet, giving in tones
the most surprising revelations from those unknown regions,
about that "laughing nymph"* of whom he demanded news: "If
she still continued to drape her silvery veil around the flowing

---

*Heine. *Saloon—Chopin.*

locks of her green hair, with a coquetry so enticing?" Familiar with the tittle-tattle and love tales of those distant lands he asked: "If the old marine god, with the long white beard, still pursued this mischievous naiad with his ridiculous love?" Fully informed, too, about all the exquisite fairy scenes to be seen *down there—down there,* he asked "if the roses always glowed there with a flame so triumphant? if the trees at moonlight sang always so harmoniously?" When Chopin had answered, and they had for a long time conversed together about that aerial clime, they would remain in gloomy silence, seized with that *mal du pays* from which Heine suffered when he compared himself to that Dutch captain of the phantom ship, with his crew eternally driven about upon the chill waves, and "sighing in vain for the spices, the tulips, the hyacinths, the pipes of sea-foam, the porcelain cups of Holland. . . . 'Amsterdam! Amsterdam! when shall we again see Amsterdam!' they cry from on board, while the tempest howls in the cordage, beating them forever about in their watery hell." Heine adds: "I fully understand the passion with which the unfortunate captain once exclaimed: 'Oh if I should *ever* again see Amsterdam! I would rather be chained forever at the corner of one of its streets, than be forced to leave it again!' Poor Van der Decken!"

Heine well knew what poor Van der Decken had suffered in his terrible and eternal course upon the ocean, which had fastened its fangs in the wood of his incorruptible vessel, and by an invisible anchor, whose chain he could not break because it could never be found, held it firmly linked upon the waves of its restless bosom. He could describe to us when he chose, the hope, the despair, the torture of the miserable beings peopling this unfortunate ship, for he had mounted its accursed timbers, led on and guided by the hand of some enamored Undine, who, when the guest of her forest of coral and palace of pearl rose more morose, more satirical, more bitter than usual, offered for the amusement of his ill humor between the repasts, some spectacle worthy of a lover who could create more wonders in his dreams than her whole kingdom contained.

Heine had traveled round the poles of the earth in this imperishable vessel; he had seen the brilliant visitor of the long nights, the aurora borealis, mirror herself in the immense stalactites of eternal ice, rejoicing in the play of colors alternating with each other in the varying folds of her glowing scarf. He had visited the tropics, where the zodiacal triangle, with its celestial light, replaces, during the short nights, the burning rays of an oppressive sun. He had crossed the latitudes where life becomes pain, and advanced into those in which it is a living death, making himself familiar, on the long way, with the heavenly miracles in the wild path of sailors who make for no port! Seated on a poop without a helm, his eye had ranged from the two Bears majestically overhanging the North, to the brilliant Southern Cross, through the blank Antarctic deserts extending through the empty space of the heavens overhead, as well as over the dreary waves below, where the despairing eye finds nothing to contemplate in the sombre depths of a sky without a star, vainly arching over a shoreless and bottomless sea! He had long followed the glittering yet fleeting traces left by the meteors through the blue depths of space; he had tracked the mystic and incalculable orbits of the comets as they flash through their wandering paths, solitary and incomprehensible, everywhere dreaded for their ominous splendor, yet inoffensive and harmless. He had gazed upon the shining of that distant star, Aldebaran, which, like the glitter and sullen glow in the eye of a vengeful enemy, glares fiercely upon our globe, without daring to approach it. He had watched the radiant planets shedding upon the restless eye which seeks them a consoling and friendly light, like the weird cabala of an enigmatic yet hopeful promise.

Heine had seen all these things, under the varying appearances which they assume in different latitudes; he had seen much more also with which he would entertain us under strange similitudes. He had assisted at the furious cavalcade of "Herodiade"; he had also an entrance at the court of the king of "Aulnes" in the gardens of the "Hesperides"; and indeed into all those places inaccessible to mortals who have not had a fairy as godmother, who would take upon herself the task of counterbalancing all the evil experienced in life, by showering upon the adopted the whole store of fairy treasures.

Upon that evening which we are now describing, Meyerbeer was seated next to Heine;—Meyerbeer, for whom the whole

catalogue of admiring interjections has long since been exhausted! Creator of Cyclopean harmonics as he was, he passed the
time in delight when following the detailed arabesques, which,
woven in transparent gauze, wound in filmy veils around the
delicate conceptions of Chopin.

Adolphe Nourrit, a noble artist, at once ascetic and passionate, was also there. He was a sincere, almost a devout Catholic,
dreaming of the future with the fervor of the Middle Ages, who,
during the latter part of his life, refused the assistance of his talent to any scene of merely superficial sentiment. He served Art
with a high and enthusiastic respect; he considered it, in all its
divers manifestations, only a holy tabernacle, "the Beauty of
which formed the splendor of the True." Already undermined
by a melancholy passion for the Beautiful, his brow seemed to
be turning into stone under the dominion of this haunting feeling: a feeling always explained by the outbreak of despair, too
late for remedy from man—man, alas! so eager to explore the
secrets of the heart—so dull to divine them!

Hiller, whose talent was allied to Chopin's, and who was one
of his most intimate friends, was there also. In advance of the
great compositions which he afterwards published, of which the
first was his remarkable Oratorio, "The Destruction of
Jerusalem," he wrote some pieces for the Piano. Among these,
those known under the title of *Etudes*, (vigorous sketches of the
most finished design), recall those studies of foliage, in which
the landscape painter gives us an entire little poem of light and
shade, with only one tree, one branch, a single "motif," happily
and boldly handled.

In the presence of the spectres which filled the air, and whose
rustling might almost be heard, Eugène Delacroix remained
absorbed and silent. Was he considering what pallet, what
brushes, what canvas he must use, to introduce them into visible life through his art? Did he task himself to discover canvas
woven by Arachne, brushes made from the long eyelashes of the
fairies, and a pallet covered with the vaporous tints of the rainbow, in order to make such a sketch possible? Did he then smile
at these fancies, yet gladly yield to the impressions from which
they sprung, because great talent is always attracted by that
power in direct contrast to its own?

The aged Niemcevicz, who appeared to be the nearest to the grave among us, listened to the *Historic Songs* which Chopin translated into dramatic execution for this survivor of times long past. Under the fingers of the Polish artist, again were heard, side by side with the descriptions, so popular, of the Polish bard, the shock of arms, the songs of conquerors, the hymns of triumph, the complaints of illustrious prisoners, and the wail over dead heroes. They memorized together the long course of national glory, of victory, of kings, of queens, of warriors; and so much life had these phantoms, that the old man, deeming the present an illusion, believed the olden times fully resuscitated.

Dark and silent, apart from all others, fell the motionless profile of Mickiewicz: the Dante of the North, he seemed always to find "the salt of the stranger bitter, and his steps hard to mount."

Buried in a fauteuil, with her arms resting upon a table, sat Madame Sand, curiously attentive, gracefully subdued. Endowed with that rare faculty only given to a few elect, of recognizing the Beautiful under whatever form of nature or of art it may assume, she listened with the whole force of her ardent genius. The faculty of instantaneously recognizing Beauty may perhaps be the "second sight," of which all nations have acknowledged the existence in highly gifted women. It is a kind of magical gaze which causes the bark, the mask, the gross envelope of form, to fall off; so that the invisible essence, the soul which is incarnated within, may be clearly contemplated; so that the ideal which the poet or artist may have vivified under the torrent of notes, the passionate veil of coloring, the cold chiseling of marble, or the mysterious rhythms of strophes, may be fully discerned. This faculty is much rarer than is generally supposed. It is usually felt but vaguely, yet—in its highest manifestations, it reveals itself as a "divining oracle," knowing the Past and prophesying the Future. It is a power which exempts the blessed organization which it illumes, from the bearing of the heavy burden of technicalities, with which the merely scientific drag on toward that mystic region of inner life, which the gifted attain with a single bound. It is a faculty which springs less from an acquaintance with the sciences, than from a familiarity with nature.

The fascination and value of a country life consist in the long *tête-à-tête* with nature. The words of revelation hidden under the infinite harmonies of form, of sounds, of lights and shadows, of tones and warblings, of terror and delight, may best be caught in these long solitary interviews. Such infinite variety may appear crushing or distracting on a first view, but if faced with a courage that no mystery can appal, if sounded with a resolution that no length of time can abate, may give the clue to analogies, conformities, relations between our senses and our sentiments, and aid us in tracing the hidden links which bind apparent dissimilarities, identical oppositions and equivalent antitheses, and teach us the secrets of the chasms separating with narrow but impassable space, that which is destined to approach forever, yet never mingle; to resemble ever, yet never blend. To have awakened early, as did Madame Sand, to the dim whispering with which nature initiates her chosen to her mystic rites, is a necessary appanage of the poet. To have learned from her to penetrate the dreams of man when he, in his turn, creates, and uses in his works the tones, the warblings, the terrors, the delights, requires a still more subtle power; a power which Madame Sand possesses by a double right, by the intuitions of her heart, and the vigor of her genius. After having named Madame Sand, whose energetic personality and electric genius inspired the frail and delicate organization of Chopin with an intensity of admiration which consumed him, as a wine too spirituous shatters the fragile vase; we cannot now call up other names from the dim limbus of the past, in which so many indistinct images, such doubtful sympathies, such indefinite projects and uncertain beliefs, are forever surging and hurtling. Perhaps there is no one among us, who, in looking through the long vista, would not meet the ghost of some feeling whose shadowy form he would find impossible to pass! Among the varied interests, the burning desires, the restless tendencies surging through the epoch in which so many high hearts and brilliant intellects were fortuitously thrown together, how few of them, alas! possessed sufficient vitality to enable them to resist the numberless causes of death, surrounding every idea, every feeling, as well as every individual life, from the cradle to the grave! Even during the moments of the troubled existence of the emotions now past,

how many of them escaped that saddest of all human judg-
ments: "Happy, oh, happy were it dead! Far happier had it never
been born!" Among the varied feelings with which so many
noble hearts throbbed high, were there indeed many which
never incurred this fearful malediction? Like the suicide lover
in Mickiewicz's poem, who returns to life in the land of the
Dead only to renew the dreadful suffering of his earth life, perhaps among all the emotions then so vividly felt there is not a
single one which, could it again live, would reappear without the
disfigurements, the brandings, the bruises, the mutilations,
which were inflicted on its early beauty, which so deeply sullied
its primal innocence! And if we should persist in recalling these
melancholy ghosts of dead thoughts and buried feelings from
the heavy folds of the shroud, would they not actually appall us,
because so few of them possessed sufficient purity and celestial
radiance to redeem them from the shame of being utterly dis-
owned, entirely repudiated, by those whose bliss or torment
they formed during the passionate hours of their absolute rule?
In very pity ask us not to call from the Dead, ghosts whose resurrection would be so painful! Who could bear the sepulchral
ghastly array? Who would willingly call them from their sheeted
sleep? If our ideas, thoughts, and feelings were indeed to be
suddenly aroused from the unquiet grave in which they lie
buried, and an account demanded from them of the good and
evil which they have severally produced in the hearts in which
they found so generous an asylum, and which they have confused, overwhelmed, illumined, devastated, ruined, broken, as
chance or destiny willed,—who could hope to endure the
replies that would be made to questions so searching?

If among the group of which we have spoken, every member
of which has won the attention of many human souls, and must,
in consequence, bear in his conscience the sharp sting of multiplied responsibilities, there should be found *one* who has not
suffered aught, that was pure in the natural attraction which
bound them together in this chain of glittering links, to fall into
dull forgetfulness; one who allowed no breath of the fermenta-
tion lingering even around the most delicate perfumes, to
embitter his memories; one who has transfigured and left to the

immortality of art, only the unblemished inheritance of all that was noblest in their enthusiasm, all that was purest and most lasting of their joys; let us bow before him as before one of the Elect! Let us regard him as one of those whom the belief of the people marks as "Good Genii!" The attribution of superior power to beings believed to be beneficent to man, has received a sublime conformation from a great Italian poet, who defines genius as a "stronger impress of Divinity!" Let us bow before all who are marked with this mystic seal; but let us venerate with the deepest, truest tenderness those who have only used their wondrous supremacy to give life and expression to the highest and most exquisite feelings! and among the pure and beneficent genii of earth must indubitably be ranked the artist Chopin!

CHAPTER V.

The Lives of Artists—Pure Fame of Chopin—Reserve—Classic and Romantic
Art—Language of the Slavs—Chopin's Love of Home—Memories

A NATURAL curiosity is generally felt to know something of the lives of men who have consecrated their genius to embellish noble feelings through works of art, through which they shine like brilliant meteors in the eyes of the surprised and delighted crowd. The admiration and sympathy awakened by the compositions of such men, attach immediately to their own names, which are at once elevated as symbols of nobility and greatness, because the world is loath to believe that those who can express high sentiments with force, can themselves feel ignobly. The objects of this benevolent prejudice, this favorable presumption, are expected to justify such suppositions by the high course of life which they are required to lead. When it is seen that the poet feels with such exquisite delicacy all that which it is so sweet to inspire; that he divines with such rapid intuition all that pride, timidity, or weariness struggles to hide; that he can paint love as youth dreams it, but as riper years despair to realize it; when such sublime situations seem to be ruled by his genius, which raises itself so calmly above the calamities of human destiny, always finding the leading threads by which the most complicated knots in the tangled skein of life may be proudly and victoriously unloosed; when the secret modulations of the most exquisite tenderness, the most heroic courage, the most sublime simplicity, are known to be subject to his command,—it is most natural that the inquiry should be made if this wondrous divination springs from a sincere faith in the reality of the noble feelings portrayed, or whether its source is to be found in an acute perception of the intellect, an abstract comprehension of the logical reason.

The question in what the life led by men so enamored of beauty differs from that of the common multitude, is then earnestly asked. This high poetic disdain,—how did it comport itself when struggling with material interests? These ineffable emotions of ethereal love,—how were they guarded from the bitterness of petty cares, from that rapidly growing and corroding mould which usually stifles or poisons them? How many of such feelings were preserved from that subtle evaporation which robs them of their perfume, that gradually increasing inconstancy which lulls us until we forget to call the dying emotions to account? Those who felt such holy indignation,—were they indeed always just? Those who exalted integrity,—were they always equitable? Those who sung of honor,—did they never stoop? Those who so admired fortitude,—have they never compromised with their own weakness?

A deep interest is also felt in ascertaining how those to whom the task of sustaining our faith in the nobler sentiments through art has been intrusted, have conducted themselves in external affairs, where pecuniary gain is only to be acquired at the expense of delicacy, loyalty, or honor. Many assert that the nobler feelings exist only in the works of art. When some unfortunate occurrence seems to give a deplorable foundation to the words of such mockers, with what avidity they name the most exquisite conceptions of the poet, "vain phantoms!" How they plume themselves upon their own wisdom in having advocated the politic doctrine of an astute, yet honeyed hypocrisy; how they delight to speak of the perpetual contradiction between words and deeds! . . . . With what cruel joy they detail such occurrences, and cite such examples in the presence of those unsteady restless souls, who are incited by their youthful aspirations and by the depression and utter loss of happy confidence which such a conviction would entail upon them, to struggle against a distrust so blighting! When such wavering spirits are engaged in the bitter combat with the harsh alternatives of life, or tempted at every turn by its insinuating seductions, what a profound discouragement seizes upon them when they are induced to believe that the hearts devoted to the most sublime

thoughts, the most deeply initiated in the most delicate susceptibilities, the most charmed by the beauty of innocence, have
denied, by their acts, the sincerity of their worship for the noble
themes which they have sung as poets! With what agonizing
doubts are they not filled by such flagrant contradictions! How
much is their anguish increased by the jeering mockery of those
who repeat: "Poetry is only that which might have been"—and
who delight in blaspheming it by their guilty negations!
Whatever may be the human short-comings of the gifted,
believe the truths they sing! Poetry is more than the gigantic
shadow of our own imagination, immeasurably increased, and
projected upon the flying plane of the Impossible. *Poetry* and
Reality are not two incompatible elements, destined to move on
together without commingling. Goethe himself confesses this.
In speaking of a contemporary writer he says: "that having lived
to create poems, he had also made his life a Poem." (*Er lebte
dichtend, und dichtete lebend.*) Goethe was himself too true a
poet not to know that Poetry only is, because its eternal Reality
throbs in the noble impulses of the human heart.

We have once before remarked that "genius imposes its own
obligations."° If the examples of cold austerity and of rigid disinterestedness are sufficient to awaken the admiration of calm
and reflective natures, whence shall more passionate and
mobile organizations, to whom the dullness of mediocrity is
insipid, who naturally seek honor or pleasure, and who are willing to purchase the object of their desires at any price—form
their models? Such temperaments easily free themselves from
the authority of their seniors. They do not admit their compe-
tency to decide. They accuse them of wishing to use the world
only for the profit of their own dead passions, of striving to turn
all to their own advantage, of pronouncing upon the effects of
causes which they do not understand, of desiring to promulgate
laws in spheres to which nature has denied them entrance. They
will not receive answers from their lips, but turn to others to
resolve their doubts; they question those who have drunk deeply

---

° Upon Paganini, after his death.

from the boiling springs of grief, bursting from the riven clefts in the steep cliffs upon the top of which alone the soul seeks rest and light. They pass in silence by the still cold gravity of those who practice the good, without enthusiasm for the beautiful. What leisure has ardent youth to interpret their gravity, to resolve their chill problems? The throbbings of its impetuous heart are too rapid to allow it to investigate the hidden sufferings, the mystic combats, the solitary struggles, which may be detected even in the calm eye of the man who practices only the good. Souls in continual agitation seldom interpret aright the calm simplicity of the just, or the heroic smiles of the stoic. For them enthusiasm and emotion are necessities. A bold image persuades them, a metaphor leads them, tears convince them, they prefer the conclusions of impulse, of intuition, to the fatigue of logical argument. Thus they turn with an eager curiosity to the poets and artists who have moved them by their images, allured them by their metaphors, excited them by their enthusiasm. They demand from them the explanation, the purpose of this enthusiasm, the secret of this beauty!

When distracted by heart-rending events, when tortured by intense suffering, when feeling and enthusiasm seem to be but a heavy and cumbersome load which may upset the life-boat if not thrown overboard into the abyss of forgetfulness; who, when menaced with utter shipwreck after a long struggle with peril, has not evoked the glorious shades of those who have conquered, whose thoughts glow with noble ardor, to inquire from them how far their aspirations were sincere, how long they preserved their vitality and truth? Who has not exerted an ingenious discernment to ascertain how much of the generous feeling depicted was only for mental amusement, a mere speculation; how much had really become incorporated with the habitual acts of life? Detraction is never idle in such cases; it seizes eagerly upon the foibles, the neglect, the faults of those who have been degraded by any weakness: alas, it omits nothing! It chases its prey, it accumulates facts only to distort them, it arrogates to itself the right of despising the inspiration to which it will grant no authority or aim but to furnish amusement, denying it any claim to guide our actions, our resolutions, our refusal, our consent! Detraction knows well how to winnow history! Casting aside all the good grain, it carefully gathers all the tares, to scatter the black seed over the brilliant pages in which the purest desires of the heart, the noblest dreams of the imagination are found; and with the irony of assumed victory, demands what the grain is worth which only germinates dearth and famine? Of what value the vain words, which only nourish sterile feelings? Of what use are excursions into realms in which no real fruit can ever be gathered? of what possible importance are emotions and enthusiasm, which always end in calculations of interest, covering only with brilliant veil the covert struggles of egotism and venal self-interest?

With how much arrogant derision men given to such detraction, contrast the noble thoughts of the poet, with his unworthy acts! The high compositions of the artist, with his guilty frivolity! What a haughty superiority they assume over the laborious merit of the men of guileless honesty, whom they look upon as crustacea, sheltered from temptation by the immobility of weak organizations, as well as over the pride of those, who, believing themselves superior to such temptations, do not, they assert, succeed even as well as themselves in repudiating the pursuit of material well being, the gratification of vanity, or the pleasure of immediate enjoyment! What an easy triumph they win over the hesitation, the doubt, the repugnance of those who would fain cling to a belief in the possibility of the union of vivid feelings, passionate impressions, intellectual gifts, imaginative temperaments, with high integrity, pure lives, and courses of conduct in perfect harmony with poetic ideals!

It is therefore impossible not to feel the deepest sadness when we meet with any fact which shows us the poet disobedient to the inspiration of the Muses, those guardian angels of the man of genius, who would willingly teach him to make of his own life the most beautiful of poems. What disastrous doubts in the minds of others, what profound discouragements, what melancholy apostasies are induced by the faltering steps of the man of genius! And yet it would be profanity to confound his errors in the same anathema, hurled against the base vices of meanness, the shameless effrontery of low crime! It would be sacrilege! If the acts of the poet have sometimes denied the spirit of his song, have not his songs still more powerfully denied his acts? May not the limited influence of his private actions have been far more than counterbalanced by the germs of creative virtues, scattered profusely through his eloquent writings? Evil is contagious, but good is truly fruitful! The poet, even while forcing his inner convictions to give way to his personal interest, still acknowledges and ennobles the sentiments which condemn himself; such sentiments attain a far wider influence through his works than can be exerted by his individual acts. Are not the number of spirits which have been calmed, consoled, edified, through these works, far greater than the number of those who have been injured by the errors of his private life? Art is far more powerful than the artist. His creations have a life independent of his vacillating will; for they are revelations of the "immutable beauty!" More durable than himself, they pass on from generation to generation; let us hope that they may, through the blessings of their widely spread influence, contain a virtual power of redemption for the frequent errors of their gifted authors.

If it be indeed true that many of those who have immortalized their sensibility and their aspirations, by robing them in the garb of surpassing eloquence, have, nevertheless, stifled these high aspirations, abused these quick sensibilities,—how many have they not confirmed, strengthened and encouraged to pursue a noble course, through the works created by their genius! A generous indulgence towards them would be but justice! It is hard to be forced to claim simple justice for them; unpleasant to be constrained to defend those whom we wish to be admired, to excuse those whom we wish to see venerated!

With what exultant feelings of just pride may the friend and artist remember a career in which there are no jarring dissonances; no contradictions, for which he is forced to claim indulgence; no errors, whose source must be found in palliation of their existence; no extreme, to be accounted for as the consequence of "excess of cause." How sweet it is to be able to name one who has fully proved that it is not only apathetic beings whom no fascination can attract, no illusion betray, who are able to limit themselves within the strict routine of honored and honorable laws, who may justly claim that elevation of soul, which no reverse subdues, and which is never found in contradiction with its better self! Doubly dear and doubly honored must the

memory of Chopin, in this respect, ever remain! Dear to the
friends and artists who have known him in his lifetime, dear to
the unknown friends who shall learn to love him through his
poetic song, as well as to the artists who, in succeeding him,
shall find their glory in being worthy of him!

The character of Chopin, in none of its numerous folds, concealed a single movement, a single impulse, which was not
dictated by the nicest sense of honor, the most delicate appreciation of affection. Yet no nature was ever more formed to justify eccentricity, whims, and abrupt caprices. His imagination was
ardent, his feelings almost violent, his physical organization
weak, irritable and sickly. Who can measure the amount of suffering arising from such contrasts? It must have been bitter, but
he never allowed it to be seen! He kept the secret of his tor-
ments, he veiled them from all eyes under the impenetrable
serenity of a haughty resignation.

The delicacy of his heart and constitution imposed upon him
the woman's torture, that of enduring agonies never to be confessed, thus giving to his fate some of the darker hues of feminine destiny. Excluded, by the infirm state of his health, from
the exciting arena of ordinary activity, without any taste for the
useless buzzing, in which a few bees, joined with many wasps,
expend their superfluous strength, he built apart from all noisy
and frequented routes a secluded cell for himself. Neither
adventures, embarrassments, nor episodes, mark his life, which
he succeeded in simplifying, although surrounded by circumstances which rendered such a result difficult of attainment. His
own feelings, his own impressions, were his events; more important in his eyes than the chances and changes of external life. He
constantly gave lessons with regularity and assiduity; domestic
and daily tasks, they were given conscientiously and satisfactori-
ly. As the devout in prayer, so he poured out his soul in his compositions, expressing in them those passions of the heart, those
unexpressed sorrows, to which the pious give vent in their com-
munion with their Maker. What they never say except upon
their knees, he said in his palpitating compositions; uttering in
the language of the tones those mysteries of passion and of grief
which man has been permitted to understand without words,
because there are no words adequate for their expression.

The care taken by Chopin to avoid the zig-zags of life, to elim-
inate from it all that was useless, to prevent its crumbling into
masses without form, has deprived his own course of incident.
The vague lines and indications surrounding his figure like misty
clouds, disappear under the touch which would strive to follow
or trace their outlines. He takes part in no actions, no drama, no
entanglements, no denouements. He exercised a decisive influence upon no human being. His will never encroached upon the
desires of another, he never constrained any other spirit, or
crushed it under the domination of his own. He never tyrannized
over another heart, he never placed a conquering hand upon the
destiny of another being. He sought nothing; he would have
scorned to have made any demands. Like Tasso, he might say:

Brama assai, poco spera, e nulla chiede.

In compensation, he escaped from all ties; from the affections
which might have influenced him, or led him into more tumul-
tuous spheres. Ready to yield all, he never gave himself. Perhaps
he knew what exclusive devotion, what love without limit he was
worthy of inspiring, of understanding, of sharing! Like other
ardent and ambitious natures, he may have thought if love and
friendship are not all—they are nothing! Perhaps it would have
been more painful for him to have accepted a part, anything less
than all, than to have relinquished all, and thus to have
remained at least faithful to his impossible Ideal! If these things
have been so or not, none ever knew, for he rarely spoke of love
or friendship. He was not exacting, like those whose high claims
and just demands exceed all that we possess to offer them. The
most intimate of his acquaintances never penetrated to that
secluded fortress in which the soul, absent from his common
life, dwelt; a fortress which he so well succeeded in concealing,
that its very existence was scarcely suspected.

In his relations and intercourse with others, he always seemed
occupied in what interested them; he was cautions not to lead
them from the circle of their own personality, lest they should
intrude into his. If he gave up but little of his time to others, at
least of that which he did relinquish, he reserved none for himself. No one ever asked him to give an account of his dreams, his
wishes, or his hopes. No one seemed to wish to know what he

sighed for, what he might have conquered, if his white and tapering fingers could have linked the brazen chords of life to the golden ones of his enchanted lyre! No one had leisure to think of this in his presence. His conversation was rarely upon subjects of any deep interest. He glided lightly over all, and as he gave but little of his time, it was easily filled with the details of the day. He was careful never to allow himself to wander into digressions of which he himself might become the subject. His individuality rarely excited the investigations of curiosity, or awakened vivid scrutiny. He pleased too much to excite much reflection. The ensemble of his person was harmonious, and called for no especial commentary. His blue eye was more spiritual than dreamy, his bland smile never writhed into bitterness. The transparent delicacy of his complexion pleased the eye, his fair hair was soft and silky, his nose slightly aquiline, his bearing so distinguished, and his manners stamped with so much high breeding, that involuntarily he was always treated *en prince*. His gestures were many and graceful; the tone of his voice was veiled, often stifled; his stature was low, and his limbs slight. He constantly reminded us of a convolvulus balancing its heaven-colored cup upon an incredibly slight stem, the tissue of which is so like vapor that the slightest contact wounds and tears the misty corolla.

His manners in society possessed that serenity of mood which distinguishes those whom no ennui annoys, because they expect no interest. He was generally gay, his caustic spirit caught the ridiculous rapidly and far below the surface at which it usually strikes the eye. He displayed a rich vein of drollery in pantomime. He often amused himself by reproducing the musical formulas and peculiar tricks of certain virtuosi, in the most burlesque and comic improvisations, in imitating their gestures, their movements, in counterfeiting their faces with a talent which instantaneously depicted their whole personality. His own features would then become scarcely recognizable, he could force the strangest metamorphoses upon them, but while mimicking the ugly and grotesque, he never lost his own native grace. Grimace was never carried far enough to disfigure him; his gayety was so much the more piquant because he always restrained it within the limits of perfect good taste, holding at a suspicious distance all that could wound the most fastidious delicacy. He never made use of an inelegant word, even in the moments of the most entire familiarity; an improper merriment, a coarse jest would have been shocking to him.

Through a strict exclusion of all subjects relating to himself from conversation, through a constant reserve with regard to his own feelings, he always succeeded in leaving a happy impression behind him. People in general like those who charm them without causing them to fear that they will be called upon to render aught in return for the amusement given, or that the pleasurable excitement of gayety will be followed by the sadness of melancholy confidences the sight of mournful faces, or the inevitable reactions which occur in susceptible natures of which we may say: *Ubi mel, ibi fel.* People generally like to keep such "susceptible natures" at a distance; they dislike to be brought into contact with their melancholy moods, though they do not refuse a kind of respect to the mournful feelings caused by their subtle reactions; indeed such changes possess for them the attraction of the unknown and they are as ready to take delight in the description of such changing caprices, as they are to avoid their reality. The presence of Chopin was always fêted. He interested himself so vividly in all that was not himself, that his own personality remained intact, unapproached and unapproachable, under the polished and glassy surface upon which it was impossible to gain footing.

On some occasions, although very rarely, we have seen him deeply agitated. We have seen him grow so pale and wan, that his appearance was actually corpse-like. But even in moments of the most intense emotion, he remained concentrated within himself. A single instant for self-recovery always enabled him to veil the secret of his first impression. However full of spontaneity his bearing afterwards might seem to be, it was instantaneously the effect of reflection, of a will which governed the strange conflict of emotional and moral energy with conscious physical debility; a conflict whose strange contrasts were forever warring vividly within. The dominion exercised over the natural violence of his character reminds us of the melancholy force of those beings who seek their strength in isolation and entire self-control, conscious of the uselessness of their vivid indignation and vexation, and too jealous of the mysteries of their passions to betray them gratuitously.

He could pardon in the most noble manner. No rancor remained in his heart toward those who had wounded him, though such wounds penetrated deeply in his soul, and fermented there in vague pain and internal suffering, so that long after the exciting cause had been effaced from his memory, he still experienced the secret torture. By dint of constant effort, in spite of his acute and tormenting sensibilities, he subjected his feelings to the rule rather of what ought to be, than of what is; thus he was grateful for services proceeding rather from good intentions than from a knowledge of what would have been agreeable to him; from friendship which wounded him, because not aware of his acute but concealed susceptibility. Nevertheless the wounds caused by such awkward miscomprehension are, of all others, the most difficult for nervous temperaments to bear. Condemned to repress their vexation, such natures are excited by degrees to a state of constantly gnawing irritability, which they can never attribute to the true cause. It would be a gross mistake to imagine that this irritation existed without provocation. But as a dereliction from what appeared to him to be the most honorable course of conduct was a temptation which he was never called upon to resist, because in all probability it never presented itself to him; so he never, in the presence of the more vigorous and therefore more brusque and positive individualities than his own, unveiled the shudder, if repulsion be too strong a term, caused by their contact or association.

The reserve which marked his intercourse with others, extended to all subjects to which the fanaticism of opinion can attach. His own sentiments could only be estimated by that which he did not do in the narrow limits of his activity. His patriotism was revealed in the course taken by his genius, in the choice of his friends, in the preferences given to his pupils, and in the frequent and great services which he rendered to his compatriots; but we cannot remember that he took any pleasure in the expression of this feeling. If he sometimes entered upon the topic of politics, so vividly attacked, so warmly defended, so frequently discussed in France, it was rather to point out what he deemed dangerous or erroneous in the opinions advanced by others than to win attention for his own. In constant connection with some of the most brilliant politicians of the day, he knew how to limit the relations between them to a personal attachment entirely independent of political interests.

Democracy presented to his view an agglomeration of elements too heterogeneous, too restless, wielding too much savage power, to win his sympathies. The entrance of social and political questions into the arena of popular discussion was compared, more than twenty years ago, to a new and bold incursion of barbarians. Chopin was peculiarly and painfully struck by the terror which this comparison awakened. He despaired of obtaining the safety of Rome from these modern Attilas, he feared the destruction of art, its monuments, its refinements, its civilization; in a word, he dreaded the loss of the elegant, cultivated if somewhat indolent ease described by Horace. Would the graceful elegancies of life, the high culture of the arts, indeed be safe in the rude and devastating hands of the new barbarians? He followed at a distance the progress of events, and an acuteness of perception, which he would scarcely have been supposed to possess, often enabled him to predict occurrences which were not anticipated even by the best informed. But though such observations escaped him, he never developed them. His concise remarks attracted no attention until time proved their truth. His good sense, full of acuteness, had early persuaded him of the perfect vacuity of the greater part of political orations, of theological discussions, of philosophic digressions. He began early to practice the favorite maxim of a man of great distinction, whom we have often heard repeat a remark dictated by the misanthropic wisdom of age, which was then startling to our inexperienced impetuosity, but which has since frequently struck us by its melancholy truth: "You will be persuaded one day as I am," (said the Marquis de Noailles to the young people whom he honored with his attention, and who were becoming heated in some naïve discussions of differing opinions,) "that it is scarcely possible to talk about anything to any body." (*Qu'il n'y a guère moyen de causer de quoi que ce soit, avec qui que ce soit.*)

Sincerely religious, and attached to Catholicity, Chopin never touched upon this subject, but held his faith without attracting attention to it. One might have been acquainted with him for a long time, without knowing exactly what his religious opinions were. Perhaps to console his inactive hand and reconcile it with his lute, he persuaded himself to think: *Il mondo va da se.* We have frequently watched him during the progress of long, animated, and stormy discussions, in which he would take no part. In the excitement of the debate he was forgotten by the speakers, but we have often neglected to follow the chain of their reasoning, to fix our attention upon the features of Chopin, which were almost imperceptibly contracted when subjects touching upon the most important conditions of our existence were discussed with such eagerness and ardor, that it might have been thought our fates were to be instantly decided by the result of the debate. At such times, he appeared to us like a passenger on board of a vessel, driven and tossed by tempests upon the stormful waves, thinking of his distant country, watching the horizon, the stars, the manœuvres of the sailors, counting their fatal mistakes, without possessing in himself sufficient force to seize a rope, or the energy requisite to haul in a fluttering sail.

On one single subject he relinquished his premeditated silence, his cherished neutrality. In the cause of art he broke through his reserve, he never abdicated upon this topic the explicit enunciation of his opinions. He applied himself with great perseverance to extend the limits of his influence upon this subject. It was a tacit confession that he considered himself legitimately possessed of the authority of a great artist. In questions which he dignified by his competence, he never left any doubt with regard to the nature of his opinions. During several years his appeals were full of impassioned ardor, but later, the triumph of his opinions having diminished the interest of his rôle, he sought no further occasion to place himself as leader, as the bearer of any banner. In the only occurrence in which he took part in the conflict of parties, he gave proof of opinions, absolute, tenacious, and inflexible, as those which rarely come to the light usually are.

Shortly after his arrival in Paris, in 1832, a new school was formed both in literature and music, and youthful talent appeared, which shook off with eclat the yoke of ancient formulas. The scarcely lulled political effervescence of the first years of the revolution of July, passed into questions upon art and letters, which attracted the attention and interest of all minds. *Romanticism* was the order of the day; they fought with obstinacy for and against it. What truce could there be between those who would not admit the possibility of writing in any other than the already established manner, and those who thought that the artist should be allowed to choose such forms as he deemed best suited for the expression of his ideas; that the rule of form should be found in the agreement of the chosen form with the sentiments to be expressed, every different shade of feeling requiring of course a different mode of expression? The former believed in the existence of a permanent form, whose perfection represented absolute Beauty. But in admitting that the great masters had attained the highest limits in art, had reached supreme perfection, they left to the artists who succeeded them no other glory than the hope of approaching these models, more or less closely, by imitation, thus frustrating all hope of ever equalling them, because the perfecting of any process can never rival the merit of its invention. The latter denied that the immaterial Beautiful could have a fixed and absolute form. The different forms which had appeared in the history of art, seemed to them like tents spread in the interminable route of the ideal; mere momentary halting places which genius attains from epoch to epoch, and beyond which the inheritors of the past should strive to advance. The former wished to restrict the creations of times and natures the most dissimilar, within the limits of the same symmetrical frame; the latter claimed for all writers the liberty of creating their own mode, accepting no other rules than those which result from the direct relation of sentiment and form, exacting only that the form should be adequate to the expression of the sentiment. However admirable the existing models might be, they did not appear to them to have exhausted all the range of sentiments upon which art might seize, or all the forms which it might advantageously use. Not contented with the mere excellence of form, they sought it so far only as its perfection is indispensable for the complete revelation of the idea, for they were not ignorant that the sentiment is maimed if the form remain imperfect, any imperfection in it, like an opaque veil, intercepting the raying of the pure idea. Thus they elevated what had otherwise been the mere work of the trade, into the sphere of poetic inspiration. They enjoined upon genius and patience the task of inventing a form which would satisfy the exactions of the inspiration. They reproached their adversaries with attempting to reduce inspiration to the bed of Procrustes, because they refused to admit that there are sentiments which cannot be expressed in forms which have been determined upon beforehand, and of thus robbing art, in advance even of their creation, of all works which might attempt the introduction of newly awakened ideas, newly clad in new forms; forms and ideas both naturally arising from the naturally progressive development of the human spirit, the improvement of the instruments, and the consequent increase of the material resources of art.

Those who saw the flames of Genius devour the old worm-eaten crumbling skeletons, attached themselves to the musical school of which the most gifted, the most brilliant, the most daring representative, was Berlioz. Chopin joined this school. He persisted most strenuously in freeing himself from the servile formulas of conventional style, while he earnestly repudiated the charlatanism which sought to replace the old abuses only by the introduction of new ones.

During the years which this campaign of Romanticism lasted, in which some of the trial blows were master-strokes, Chopin remained invariable in his predilections, as well as in his repulsions. He did not admit the least compromise with those who, in his opinion, did not sufficiently represent progress, and who, in their refusal to relinquish the desire of displaying art for the profit of the trade, in their pursuit of transitory effects, of success won only from the astonishment of the audience, gave no proof of sincere devotion to progress. He broke the ties which he had contracted with respect when he felt restricted by them, or bound too closely to the shore by cordage which he knew to be decayed. He obstinately refused, on the other hand, to form ties with the young artists whose success, which he deemed exaggerated, elevated a certain kind of merit too highly. He never gave the least praise to anything which he did not believe to be a real conquest for art, or which did not evince a serious conception of the task of an artist. He did not wish to be lauded by any party, to be aided by the manœuvres of any faction, or by the concessions made by any schools in the persons of their chiefs. In the midst of jealousies, encroachments, forfeitures, and invasions of the different branches of art, negotiations, treaties, and contracts have been introduced, like the means and appliances of diplomacy, with all the artifices inseparable from such a course. In refusing the support of any accessory aid for his productions, he proved that he confidently believed that their own beauty would ensure their appreciation, and that he did not struggle to facilitate their immediate reception.

He supported our struggles, at that time so full of uncertainty, when we met more sages shaking their heads, than glorious adversaries, with his calm and unalterable conviction. He aided us with opinions so fixed that neither weariness nor artifice could shake them, with a rare immutability of will, and that efficacious assistance which the creation of meritorious works always brings to a struggling cause, when it can claim them as its own. He mingled so many charms, so much moderation, so much knowledge with his daring innovations, that the prompt admiration he inspired fully justified the confidence he placed in his own genius. The solid studies which he had made, the reflective habits of his youth, the worship for classic models in which he had been educated, preserved him from losing his strength in blind gropings, in doubtful triumphs, as has happened to more than one partisan of the new ideas. His studious patience in the elaboration of his works sheltered him from the critics, who envenomed the dissensions by seizing upon those easy and insignificant victories due to omissions, and the negligence of inadvertence. Early trained to the exactions and restrictions of rules, having produced compositions filled with beauty when subjected to all their fetters, he never shook them off without an appropriate cause and after due reflection. In virtue of his principles he always progressed, but without being led into exaggeration or lured by compromise; he willingly relinquished theoretic formulas to pursue their results. Less occupied with the disputes of the schools and their terms, than in producing himself the best argument, a finished work, he was fortunate enough to avoid personal enmities and vexatious accommodations.

Chopin had that reverential worship for art which characterized the first masters of the middle ages, but in expression and
bearing he was more simple, modern, and less ecstatic. As for
them, so art was for him, a high and holy vocation. Like them he
was proud of his election for it, and honored it with devout piety.
This feeling was revealed at the hour of his death through an
occurrence, the significance of which is more fully explained by
a knowledge of the manners prevalent in Poland. By a custom
which still exists, although it is now falling into disuse, the Poles
often chose the garments in which they wished to be buried,
and which were frequently prepared a long time in advance.°
Their dearest wishes were thus expressed for the last time, their
inmost feelings were thus at the hour of death betrayed.
Monastic robes were frequently chosen by worldly men, the
costumes of official charges were selected or refused as the
remembrances connected with them were glorious or painful.
Chopin, who, although among the first of contemporary artists,
had given the fewest concerts, wished, notwithstanding, to be
borne to the grave in the clothes which he had worn on such
occasions. A natural and profound feeling springing from the
inexhaustible sources of art, without doubt dictated this dying
request, when having scrupulously fulfilled the last duties of a
Christian, he left all of earth which he could not bear with him
to the skies. He had linked his love for art and his faith in it with
immortality long before the approach of death, and as he robed
himself for his long sleep in the grave, he gave, as was custom-
ary with him, by a mute symbol, the last touching proof of the
conviction he had preserved intact during the whole course of
his life. Faithful to himself, he died adoring art in its mystic
greatness, its highest revelations.

In retiring from the turmoil of society, Chopin concentrated
his cares and affections upon the circle of his own family and his

---

°General K——, the author of *Julie and Adolphe,* a romance imitated from the
New Heloïse which was much in vogue at the time of its publication, and who
was still living in Volhynia at the date of our visit to Poland, though more than
eighty years of age, in conformity with the custom spoken of above, had
caused his coffin to be made, and for more than thirty years it had always
stood at the door of his chamber.

early acquaintances. Without any interruption he preserved close relations with them; never ceasing to keep them up with the greatest care. His sister Louise was especially dear to him, a resemblance in the character of their minds, the bent of their feelings, bound them closely to each other. Louise frequently came from Warsaw to Paris to see him. She spent the last three months of his life with the brother she loved, watching over him with undying affection.

Chopin kept up a regular correspondence with the members of his own family, but only with them. It was one of his peculiarities to write letters to no others; it might almost have been thought that he had made a vow to write to no strangers. It was curious enough to see him resort to all kinds of expedients to escape the necessity of tracing the most insignificant note. Many times he has traversed Paris from one end to the other, to decline an invitation to dinner, or to give some trivial information, rather than write a few lines which would have spared him all this trouble and loss of time. His handwriting was quite unknown to the greatest number of his friends. It is said he sometimes departed from this custom in favor of his beautiful countrywomen, some of whom possess several of his notes written in Polish. This infraction of what seemed to be a law with him, may be attributed to the pleasure he took in the use of this language. He always used it with the people of his own country, and loved to translate its most expressive phrases. He was a good French scholar, as the Slavs generally are. In consequence of his French origin, the language had been taught him with peculiar care. But he did not like it, he did not think it sufficiently sonorous, and he deemed its genius cold. This opinion is very prevalent among the Poles, who, although speaking it with great facility, often better than their native tongue, and frequently using it in their intercourse with each other, yet complain to those who do not speak Polish of the impossibility of rendering the thousand ethereal and shifting modes of thought in any other idiom. In their opinion it is sometimes dignity, sometimes grace, sometimes passion, which is wanting in the French language. If they are asked the meaning of a word or a phrase which they may have cited in Polish, the reply invariably is: "Oh, that cannot be translated!" Then follow explanations, serving as

comments to the exclamation, of all the subtleties, all the shades
of meaning, all the delicacies contained in *the not to be translated* words. We have cited some examples which, joined to
others, induce us to believe that this language has the advantage
of making images of abstract nouns, and that in the course of its
development, through the poetic genius of the nation, it has
been enabled to establish striking and just relations between
ideas by etymologies, derivations, and synonymes. Colored
reflections of light and shade are thus thrown upon all expressions, so that they necessarily call into vibration through the
mind the correspondent tone of a third, which modulates the
thought into a major or minor mode. The richness of the
language always permits the choice of the mode, but this very
richness may become a difficulty. It is not impossible that the
general use of foreign tongues in Poland may be attributed to
indolence of mind or want of application; may be traced to a
desire to escape the necessary labor of acquiring that mastery of
diction indispensable in a language so full of sudden depths, of
laconic energy, that it is very difficult, if not quite impossible, to
support in it the commonplace. The vague agreements of badly
defined ideas cannot be compressed in the nervous strength of
its grammatical forms; the thought, if it be really low, cannot be
elevated from its debasement or poverty; if it really soar above
the commonplace, it requires a rare precision of terms not to
appear uncouth or fantastic. In consequence of this, in proportion to the works published, the Polish literature should be able
to show a greater number of *chefs-d'œuvre* than can be done in
any other language. He who ventures to use this tongue, must
feel himself already master.* Chopin mingled a charming grace

---

*It cannot be reproached with a want of harmony or musical charm. The
harshness of a language does not always and absolutely depend upon the
number of consonants, but rather upon the manner of their association. We
might even assert, that in consequence of the absence of well-determined
and strongly marked sounds, some languages have a dull and cold coloring. It
is the frequent repetition of certain consonants which gives shadow, rhythm,
and vigor to a tongue; the vowels imparting only a kind of light clear hue,
which requires to be brought out by deeper shades. It is the sharp, uncouth,
or unharmonious clashing of heterogeneous consonants which strikes the ear
painfully. It is true the Slavic languages make use of many consonants, but

with all the intercourse which he held with his relatives. Not satisfied with limiting his whole correspondence to them alone, he
profited by his stay in Paris to procure for them the thousand
agreeable surprises given by the novelties, the bagatelles, the little gifts which charm through their beauty, or attract as being
the first seen of their kind. He sought for all that he had reason
to believe would please his friends in Warsaw, adding constant
presents to his many letters. It was his wish that his gifts should
be preserved, that through the memories linked with them he
might be often remembered by those to whom they were sent.
He attached the greatest importance, on his side, to all the evi-
dences of their affection for him. To receive news or some mark
of their remembrance, was always a festival for him. He never
shared this pleasure with anyone, but it was plainly visible in his
conduct. He took the greatest care of every thing that came

---

their connection is generally sonorous, sometimes pleasant to the ear, and
scarcely ever entirely discordant, even when the combinations are more striking than agreeable. The quality of the sounds is rich, full, and varied. They are
not straitened and contracted as if produced in a narrow medium, but extending through a considerable register, range through a variety of intonations.
The letter L, almost impossible for those to pronounce, who have not
acquired the pronunciation in their infancy, has nothing harsh in its sound.
The ear receives from it an impression similar to that which is made upon the
fingers by the touch of a thick woolen velvet, rough, but at the same time,
yielding. The union of jarring consonants being rare, and the assonances easily multiplied, the same comparison might be employed to the ensemble of
the effect produced by these idioms upon foreigners. Many words occur in
Polish which imitate the sound of the thing designated by them. The frequent
repetition of ch, (h aspirated,) of sz, (ch in French,) of rz, of cz, so frightful to
a profane eye, have however nothing barbaric in their sounds, being pronounced nearly like geai, and tche, and greatly facilitate imitations of the
sense by the sound. The word dzwiek, (read dzwiinque,) meaning sound,
offers a characteristic example of this; it would be difficult to find a word
which would reproduce more accurately the sensation which a diapason
makes upon the ear. Among the consonants accumulated in groups, producing very different sounds, sometimes metallic, sometimes buzzing, hissing or
rumbling, many diphthongs and vowels are mingled, which sometimes
become slightly nasal, the a and e being sounded as on and in, (in French,)
when they are accompanied by a cedilla. In juxtaposition with the é, (tse,)
which is pronounced with great softness, sometimes c, (tsie,) the accented s is
almost warbled. The z has three sounds: the ż (jais,) the z, (zed,) and the

from his distant friends, the least of their gifts was precious to him, he never allowed others to make use of them, indeed he was visibly uneasy if they touched them.

Material elegance was as natural to him as mental; this was evinced in the objects with which he surrounded himself, as well as in the aristocratic grace of his manners. He was passionately fond of flowers. Without aiming at the brilliant luxury with which, at that epoch, some of the celebrities in Paris decorated their apartments, he knew how to keep upon this point, as well as in his style of dress, the instinctive line of perfect propriety.

Not wishing the course of his life, his thoughts, his time, to be associated or shackled in any way by the pursuits of others, he preferred the society of ladies, as less apt to force him into

---

z, (*zied*). The *y* forms a vowel of a muffled tone, which, as the *L*, cannot be represented by any equivalent sound in French, and which like it gives a variety of ineffable shades to the language. These fine and light elements enable the Polish women to assume a lingering and singing accent, which they usually transport into other tongues. When the subjects are serious or melancholy, after such recitatives or improvised lamentations, they have a sort of lisping infantile manner of speaking, which they vary by light silvery laughs, little interjectional cries, short musical pauses upon the higher notes, from which they descend by one knows not what chromatic scale of demi and quarter tones to rest upon some low note; and again pursue the varied, brusque and original modulations which astonish the ear not accustomed to such lovely warblings, to which they sometimes give that air of caressing irony, of cunning mockery, peculiar to the song of some birds. They love to *zinziluler*, and charming changes, piquant intervals, unexpected cadences naturally find place in this fondling prattle, making the language far more sweet and caressing when spoken by the women, than it is in the mouths of the men. The men indeed pride themselves upon speaking it with elegance, impressing upon it a masculine sonorousness, which is peculiarly adapted to the energetic movements of manly eloquence, formerly so much cultivated in Poland. Poetry commands such a diversity of prosodies, of rhymes, of rhythms, such an abundance of assonances from these rich and varied materials, that it is almost possible to follow *musically* the feelings and scenes which it depicts, not only in mere expressions in which the sound repeats the sense, but also in long declamations. The analogy between the Polish and Russian, has been compared to that which obtains between the Latin and Italian. The Russian

subsequent relations. He willingly spent whole evenings in playing blind man's buff with the young people, telling them little stories to make them break into the silvery laughs of youth, sweeter than the song of the nightingale. He was fond of a life in the country, or the life of the *château*. He was ingenious in varying its amusements, in multiplying its enjoyments. He also loved to compose there. Many of his best works written in such moments, perhaps embalm and hallow the memories of his happiest days.

---

language is indeed more mellifluous, more lingering, more caressing, fuller of sighs than the Polish. Its cadencing is peculiarly fitted for song. The finer poems, such as those of Zukowski and Pouchkin, seem to contain a melody already designated in the metre of the verses; for example, it would appear quite possible to detach an *arioso* or a sweet *cantiable* from some of the stanzas of *Le Châte noir,* or the *Talisman*. The ancient Slavonic, which is the language of the Eastern Church, possesses great majesty. More guttural than the idioms which have arisen from it, it is severe and monotonous yet of great dignity, like the Byzantine paintings preserved in the worship to which it is consecrated. It has throughout the characteristics of a sacred language which has only been used for the expression of one feeling and has never been modulated or fashioned by profane wants.

CHAPTER VI.

Birth and Early Life of Chopin—National Artists—Chopin Embodies in Himself
the Poetic Sense of his Whole Nation—Opinion of Beethoven

CHOPIN was born in 1810, at Zelazowa-Wola, near Warsaw. Unlike most other children, he could not, during his childhood, remember his own age, and the date of his birth was only fixed in his memory by a watch given him in 1820 by Madame Catalani, which bore the following inscription: "Madame Catalani to Frederic Chopin, aged ten years." Perhaps the presentiments of the artist gave to the child a foresight of his future! Nothing extraordinary marked the course of his boyhood; his internal development traversed but few phases, and gave but few manifestations. As he was fragile and sickly, the attention of his family was concentrated upon his health. Doubtless it was from this cause that he acquired his habits of affability, his patience under suffering, his endurance of every annoyance with a good grace; qualities which he early acquired from his wish to calm the constant anxiety that was felt with regard to him. No precocity of his faculties, no precursory sign of remarkable development, revealed, in his early years, his future superiority of soul, mind, or capacity. The little creature was seen suffering indeed, but always trying to smile, patient and apparently happy and his friends were so glad that he did not become moody or morose, that they were satisfied to cherish his good qualities, believing that he opened his heart to them without reserve, and gave to them all his secret thoughts. But there are souls among us who resemble rich travelers thrown among simple herdsmen, loading them with gifts during their sojourn among them, truly not at all in proportion to their own wealth, yet which are quite sufficient to astonish the poor hosts, and to spread riches and happiness in the midst of such simple habits.

It is true that such souls give as much affection, it may be more, than those who surround them; everybody is pleased with them, they are supposed to have been generous, when the truth is that in comparison with their boundless wealth they have not been liberal, and have given but little of their store of internal treasure.

The habits in which Chopin grew up, in which he was rocked as in a form-strengthening cradle, were those peculiar to calm, occupied, and tranquil characters. These early examples of simplicity, piety, and integrity, always remained the nearest and dearest to him. Domestic virtues, religious habits, pious charities, and rigid modesty, surrounded him from his infancy with that pure atmosphere in which his rich imagination assumed the velvety tenderness characterizing the plants which have never been exposed to the dust of the beaten highways.

He commenced the study of music at an early age, being but nine years old when he began to learn it. Shortly after he was confided to a passionate disciple of Sebastian Bach, Ziwna, who directed his studies during many years in accordance with the most classic models. It is not to be supposed that when he embraced the career of a musician, any prestige of vain glory, any fantastic perspective, dazzled his eyes, or excited the hopes of his family. In order to become a skillful and able master, he studied seriously and conscientiously, without dreaming of the greater or less amount of fame he would be able to obtain as the fruit of his lessons and assiduous labors.

In consequence of the generous and discriminating protection always granted by Prince Antoine Radziwill to the arts, and to genius, which he had the power of recognizing both as a man of intellect and as a distinguished artist; Chopin was early placed in one of the first colleges in Warsaw. Prince Radziwill did not cultivate music only as a simple dilettante, he was also a remarkable composer. His beautiful rendering of *Faust*, published some years ago, and executed at fixed epochs by the Academy of Song at Berlin, appears to us far superior to any other attempts which have been made to transport it into the realm of music, by its close internal appropriateness to the peculiar genius of the poem. Assisting the limited means of the family of Chopin, the

Prince made him the inestimable gift of a finished education, of which no part had been neglected. Through the person of a friend, M. Antoine Korzuchowski, whose own elevated mind enabled him to understand the requirements of an artistic career, the Prince always paid his pension from his first entrance into college, until the completion of his studies. From this time until the death of Chopin, M. Antoine Korzuchowski always held the closest relations of friendship with him.

In speaking of this period of his life, it gives us pleasure to quote the charming lines which may be applied to him more justly, than other pages in which his character is believed to have been traced, but in which we only find it distorted, and in such false proportions as are given in a profile drawn upon an elastic tissue, which has been pulled athwart, biased by contrary movements during the whole progress of the sketch.°

"Gentle, sensitive, and very lovely, at fifteen years of age he united the charms of adolescence with the gravity of a more mature age. He was delicate both in body and in mind. Through the want of muscular development he retained a peculiar beauty, an exceptional physiognomy, which had, if we may venture so to speak, neither age nor sex. It was not the bold and masculine air of a descendant of a race of Magnates, who knew nothing but drinking, hunting and making war; neither was it the effeminate loveliness of a cherub *couleur de rose.* It was more like the ideal creations with which the poetry of the middle ages adorned the Christian temples: a beautiful angel, with a form pure and slight as a young god of Olympus, with a face like that of a majestic woman filled with a divine sorrow, and as the crown of all, an expression at the same time tender and severe, chaste and impassioned.

"This expression revealed the depths of his being. Nothing could be purer, more exalted than his thoughts; nothing more tenacious, more exclusive, more intensely devoted, than his

---

°These extracts, with many that succeed them, in which the character of Chopin is described, are taken from *Lucrezia Floriana,* a novel by Madame Sand, in which the leading characters are said to be intended to represent Liszt, Chopin, and herself.—*Note of the Translator.*

affections. . . . But he could only understand that which closely resembled himself. . . . Every thing else only existed for him as a kind of annoying dream, which he tried to shake off while living with the rest of the world. Always plunged in reveries, realities displeased him. As a child he could never touch a sharp instrument without injuring himself with it; as a man, he never found himself face-to-face with a being different from himself without being wounded by the living contradiction. . . .

"He was preserved from constant antagonism by a voluntary and almost inveterate habit of never seeing or hearing anything which was disagreeable to him, unless it touched upon his personal affections. The beings who did not think as he did, were only phantoms in his eyes. As his manners were polished and graceful, it was easy to mistake his cold disdain or insurmountable aversion for benevolent courtesy. . . .

"He never spent an hour in open-hearted expansiveness, without compensating for it by a season of reserve. The moral causes which induced such reserve were too slight, too subtle, to be discovered by the naked eye. It was necessary to use the microscope to read his soul, into which so little of the light of the living ever penetrated. . . .

"With such a character, it seems strange he should have had friends: yet he had them, not only the friends of his mother who esteemed him as the noble son of a noble mother, but friends of his own age, who loved him ardently, and who were loved by him in return. . . . He had formed a high ideal of friendship; in the age of early illusions he loved to think that his friends and himself, brought up nearly in the same manner, with the same principles, would never change their opinions, and that no formal disagreement could ever occur between them. . . .

"He was externally so affectionate, his education had been so finished, and he possessed so much natural grace, that he had the gift of pleasing even where he was not personally known. His exceeding loveliness was immediately prepossessing, the delicacy of his constitution rendered him interesting in the eyes of women, the full yet graceful cultivation of his mind, the sweet and captivating originality of his conversation, gained for him the attention of the most enlightened men. Men less highly cultivated, liked him for his exquisite courtesy of manner. They were so much the more pleased with this, because, in their simplicity, they never imagined it was the graceful fulfillment of a duty into which no real sympathy entered.

"Could such people have divined the secrets of his mystic character, they would have said he was more amiable than loving—and with respect to them, this would have been true. But how could they have known that his real, though rare attachments, were so vivid, so profound, so undying? . . .

"Association with him in the details of life was delightful. He filled all the forms of friendship with an unaccustomed charm, and when he expressed his gratitude, it was with that deep emotion which recompenses kindness with usury. He willingly imagined that he felt himself every day dying; he accepted the cares of a friend, hiding from him, lest it should render him unhappy, the little time he expected to profit by them. He possessed great physical courage, and if he did not accept with the heroic recklessness of youth the idea of approaching death, at least he cherished the expectation of it with a kind of bitter pleasure . . . "

The attachment which he felt for a young lady, who never ceased to feel a reverential homage for him, may be traced back to his early youth. The tempest which in one of its sudden gusts tore Chopin from his native soil, like a bird dreamy and abstracted surprised by the storm upon the branches of a foreign tree, sundered the ties of this first love, and robbed the exile of a faithful and devoted wife, as well as disinherited him of a country. He never found the realization of that happiness of which he had once dreamed with her, though he won the glory of which perhaps he had never thought. Like the Madonnas of Luini whose looks are so full of earnest tenderness, this young girl was sweet and beautiful. She lived on calm, but sad. No doubt the sadness increased in that pure soul when she knew that no devotion tender as her own, ever came to sweeten the existence of one whom she had adored with that ingenuous submission, that exclusive devotion, that entire self-forgetfulness, naïve and sublime, which transform the woman into the angel.

Those who are gifted by nature with the beautiful, yet fatal energies of genius, and who are consequently forbidden to sacrifice the care of their glory to the exactions of their love, are probably right in fixing limits to the abnegation of their own personality. But the divine emotions due to absolute devotion, may be regretted even in the presence of the most sparkling endowments of genius. The utter submission, the disinterestedness of love, in absorbing the existence, the will, the very name of the woman in that of the man she loves, can alone authorize him in believing that he has really shared his life with her, and that his honorable love for her has given her that which no chance lover, accidentally met, could have rendered her: peace of heart and the honor of his name.

This young Polish lady, unfortunately separated from Chopin, remained faithful to his memory, to all that was left of him. She devoted herself to his parents. The father of Chopin would never suffer the portrait which she had drawn of him in the days of hope, to be replaced by another, though from the hands of a far more skillful artist. We saw the pale cheeks of this melancholy woman, glow like alabaster when a light shines through its snow, many years afterwards, when in gazing upon this picture, she met the eyes of his father.

The amiable character of Chopin won for him while at college the love of his fellow collegiates, particularly that of Prince Czetwertynski and his brothers. He often spent the vacations and days of festival with them at the house of their mother, the Princess Louise Czetwertynska, who cultivated music with a true feeling for its beauties, and who soon discovered the poet in the musician. Perhaps she was the first who made Chopin feel the charm of being understood, as well as heard. The Princess was still beautiful, and possessed a sympathetic soul united to many high qualities. Her saloon was one of the most brilliant and *recherché* in Warsaw. Chopin often met there the most distinguished women of the city. He became acquainted there with those fascinating beauties who had acquired a European celebrity, when Warsaw was so famed for the brilliancy, elegance, and grace of its society. He was introduced by the Princess Czetwertynska to the Princess of Lowicz; by her he was presented to the Countess Zamoyska; to the Princess Radziwill; to the Princess Jablonowska; enchantresses, surrounded by many beauties little less illustrious.

While still very young, he has often cadenced their steps to

the chords of his piano. In these meetings, which might almost
be called assemblies of fairies, he may often have discovered,
unveiled in the excitement of the dance, the secrets of enthusiastic and tender souls. He could easily read the hearts which
were attracted to him by friendship and the grace of his youth,
and thus was enabled early to learn of what a strange mixture of
leaven and cream of roses, of gunpowder and tears of angels, the
poetic Ideal of his nation is formed. When his wandering fingers
ran over the keys, suddenly touching some moving chords, he
could see how the furtive tears coursed down the cheeks of the
loving girl, or the young neglected wife; how they moistened the
eyes of the young men, enamored of, and eager for glory. Can
we not fancy some young beauty asking him to play a simple
prelude, then softened by the tones, leaning her rounded arm
upon the instrument to support her dreaming head, while she
suffered the young artist to divine in the dewy glitter of the lustrous eyes, the song sung by her youthful heart? Did not groups,
like sportive nymphs, throng around him, and begging him for
some waltz of giddying rapidity, smile upon him with such
wildering joyousness, as to put him immediately in unison with
the gay spirit of the dance? He saw there the chaste grace of his
brilliant countrywomen displayed in the Mazourka, and the
memories of their witching fascination, their winning reserve,
were never effaced from his soul.

In an apparently careless manner, but with that involuntary
and subdued emotion which accompanies the remembrance of
our early delights, he would sometimes remark that he first
understood the whole meaning of the feeling which is contained
in the melodies and rhythms of national dances, upon the days
in which he saw these exquisite fairies at some magic fête,
adorned with that brilliant coquetry which sparkles like electric
fire, and flashing from heart to heart, heightens love, blinds it,
or robs it of all hope. And when the muslins of India, which the
Greeks would have said were woven of air, were replaced by the
heavier folds of Venetian velvet, and the perfumed roses and
sculptured petals of the hot-house camellias gave way to the
gorgeous bouquets of the jewel caskets; it often seemed to him
that however good the orchestra might be, the dancers glided
less rapidly over the floor, that their laugh was less sonorous,

their eye less luminous, than upon those evenings in which the dance had been suddenly improvised, because he had succeeded in electrifying his audience through the magic of his performance. If he electrified them, it was because he repeated, truly in hieroglyphic tones, but yet easily understood by the initiated, the secret whispers which his delicate ear had caught from the reserved yet impassioned hearts, which indeed resemble the Fraxinella, that plant so full of burning and vivid life, that its flowers are always surrounded by a gas as subtle as inflammable. He had seen celestial visions glitter, and illusory phantoms fade in this sublimated air; he had divined the meaning of the swarms of passions which are forever buzzing in it; he knew how these hurtling emotions fluttered through the reckless human soul; how, notwithstanding their ceaseless agitation and excitement, they could intermingle, interweave, intercept each other, without once disturbing the exquisite proportions of external grace, the imposing and classic charm of manner. It was thus that he learned to prize so highly the noble and measured manners which preserve delicacy from insipidity; petty cares from wearisome trifling; conventionalism from tyranny; good taste from coldness; and which never permit the passions to resemble, as is often the case where such careful culture does not rule, those stony and calcareous vegetables whose hard and brittle growth takes a name of such sad contrast: flowers of iron (*Flos ferri*).

His early introduction into this society, in which regularity of form did not conceal petrifaction of heart, induced Chopin to think that the *convenances* and courtesies of manner, in place of being only a uniform mask, repressing the character of each individual under the symmetry of the same lines, rather serve to contain the passions without stifling them, coloring only that bald crudity of tone which is so injurious to their beauty, elevating that materialism which debases them, robbing them of that license which vulgarizes them, lowering that vehemence which vitiates them, pruning that exuberance which exhausts them, teaching the "lovers of the ideal" to unite the virtues which have sprung from a knowledge of evil, with those "which cause its very existence to be forgotten in speaking to those they love." As these visions of his youth deepened in the long perspective of memories, they gained in grace, in charm, in delight, in his eyes, fascinating him to such an extent that no reality could destroy their secret power over his imagination, rendering his repugnance more and more unconquerable to that license of allurement, that brutal tyranny of caprice, that eagerness to drink the cup of fantasy to the very dregs, that stormy pursuit of all the changes and incongruities of life, which rule in the strange mode of life known as *La Bohême*.

More than once in the history of art and literature, a poet has arisen, embodying in himself the poetic sense of a whole nation, an entire epoch, representing the types which his contemporaries pursue and strive to realize, in an absolute manner in his works: such a poet was Chopin for his country and for the epoch in which he was born. The poetic sentiments the most widely spread, yet the most intimate and inherent of his nation, were embodied and united in his imagination, and represented by his brilliant genius. Poland has given birth to many bards, some of whom rank among the first poets of the world.

Its writers are now making strenuous efforts to display in the strongest light, the most glorious and interesting facts of its history, the most peculiar and picturesque phases of its manners and customs. Chopin, differing from them in having formed no premeditated design, surpasses them all in originality. He did not determine upon, he did not seek such a result; he created no ideal *a priori*. Without having predetermined to transport himself into the past, he constantly remembered the glories of his country, he understood and sung the loves and tears of his contemporaries without having analyzed them in advance. He did not task himself, nor study to be a national musician. Like all truly national poets he sang spontaneously without premeditated design or preconceived choice all that inspiration dictated to him, as we hear it gushing forth in his songs without labor, almost without effort. He repeated in the most idealized form the emotions which had animated and embellished his youth; under the magic delicacy of his pen he displayed the Ideal, which is, if we may be permitted so to speak, the Real among his people; an Ideal really in existence among them, which everyone in general and each one in particular approaches by the one or the other of its many sides. Without assuming to do so, he collected in luminous sheaves the impressions felt everywhere

throughout his country—vaguely felt it is true, yet in fragments pervading all hearts. Is it not by this power of reproducing in a poetic formula, enchanting to the imagination of all
nations, the indefinite shades of feeling widely scattered but
frequently met among their compatriots, that the artists truly
national are distinguished?

Not without reason has the task been undertaken of collecting the melodies indigenous to every country. It appears to us it
would be of still deeper interest, to trace the influences forming
the characteristic powers of the authors most deeply inspired by
the genius of the nation to which they belong. Until the present
epoch there have been very few distinctive compositions, which
stand out from the two great divisions of the German and Italian
schools of music. But with the immense development which this
art seems destined to attain, perhaps renewing for us the glorious era of the Painters of the *Cinque Cento,* it is highly proba-
ble that composers will appear whose works will be marked by
an originality drawn from differences of organization, of races,
and of climates. It is to be presumed that we will be able to recognize the influences of the country in which they were born
upon the great masters in music, as well as in the other arts; that
we will be able to distinguish the peculiar and predominant
traits of the national genius more completely developed, more
poetically true, more interesting to study, in the pages of their
compositions than in the crude, incorrect, uncertain, vague and
tremulous sketches of the uncultured people.

Chopin must be ranked among the first musicians thus indi-
vidualizing in themselves the poetic sense of an entire nation,
not because he adopted the rhythm of *Polonaises, Mazourkas,*
and *Cracoviennes,* and called many of his works by such names,
for in so doing he would have limited himself to the multiplica-
tion of such works alone, and would always have given us the
same mode, the remembrance of the same thing; a reproduction
which would soon have grown wearisome, serving but to multiply compositions of similar form, which must have soon grown
more or less monotonous. It is because he filled these forms
with the feelings peculiar to his country, because the expression
of the national heart may be found under all the modes in which
he has written, that he is entitled to be considered a poet essen-

tially Polish. His *Preludes*, his *Nocturnes*, his *Scherzos*, his *Concertos*, his shortest as well as his longest compositions, are all filled with the national sensibility, expressed indeed in different degrees, modified and varied in a thousand ways, but always bearing the same character. An eminently subjective author, Chopin has given the same life to all his productions, animated all his works with his own spirit. All his writings are thus linked by a marked unity. Their beauties as well as their defects may be traced to the same order of emotions, to peculiar modes of feeling. The reproduction of the feelings of his people, idealized and elevated through his own subjective genius, is an essential requisite for the national poet who desires that the heart of his country should vibrate in unison with his own strains.

By the analogies of words and images, we should like to render it possible for our readers to comprehend the exquisite yet irritable sensibility peculiar to ardent yet susceptible hearts, to haughty yet deeply wounded souls. We cannot flatter ourselves that in the cold realm of words we have been able to give any idea of such ethereal odorous flames. In comparison with the vivid and delicious excitement produced by other arts, words always appear poor, cold, and arid, so that the assertion seems just: "that of all modes of expressing sentiments, words are the most insufficient." We cannot flatter ourselves with having attained in our descriptions the exceeding delicacy of touch, necessary to sketch that which Chopin has painted with hues so ethereal. All is subtle in his compositions, even the source of excitement, of passion; all open, frank, primitive impressions disappear in them; before they meet the eye, they have passed through the prism of an exacting, ingenious, and fertile imagination, and it has become difficult if not impossible to resolve them again into their primal elements. Acuteness of discernment is required to understand, delicacy to describe them. In seizing such refined impressions with the keenest discrimination, in embodying them with infinite art, Chopin has proved himself an artist of the highest order. It is only after long and patient study, after having pursued his sublimated ideas through their multiform ramifications, that we learn to admire sufficiently, to comprehend aright, the genius with which he has rendered his subtle thoughts visible and palpable, without once blunting their edge, or ever congealing their fiery flow.

He was so entirely filled with the sentiments whose most perfect types he believed he had known in his own youth, with the ideas which it alone pleased him to confide to art; he contemplated art so invariably from the same point of view, that his artistic preferences could not fail to be influenced by his early impressions. In the great models and *chefs-d'œuvre*, he only sought that which was in correspondence with his own soul. That which stood in relation to it pleased him; that which resembled it not, scarcely obtained justice from him. Uniting in himself the frequently incompatible qualities of passion and grace he possessed great accuracy of judgment, and preserved himself from all petty partiality, but he was but slightly attracted by the greatest beauties, the highest merits, when they wounded any of the phases of his poetic conceptions. Notwithstanding the high admiration which he entertained for the works of Beethoven, certain portions of them always seemed to him too rudely sculptured; their structure was too athletic to please him, their wrath seemed to him too tempestuous, their passion too overpowering, the lion-marrow which fills every member of his phases was matter too substantial for his tastes, and the Raphaelic and Seraphic profiles which are wrought into the midst of the nervous and powerful creations of this great genius, were to him almost painful from the force of the cutting contrast in which they are frequently set.

In spite of the charm which he acknowledged in some of the melodies of Schubert, he would not willingly listen to those in which the contours were too sharp for his ear, in which suffering lies naked, and we can almost feel the flesh palpitate, and hear the bones crack and crash under the rude embrace of sorrow. All savage wildness was repulsive to him. In music, in literature, in the conduct of life, all that approached the melodramatic was painful to him. The frantic and despairing aspects of exaggerated romanticism were repellent to him, he could not endure the struggling for wonderful effects, for delicious excesses. "He loved Shakspeare only under many conditions. He thought his characters were drawn too closely to the life, and spoke a language too true; he preferred the epic and lyric syntheses which leave the poor details of humanity in the shade. For the same reason he spoke little and listened less, not wishing to give expression to his own thoughts, or to receive the thoughts of others, until after they had attained a certain degree of elevation."

A nature so completely master of itself, so full of delicate reserve, which loved to divine through glimpses, presentiments, suppositions, all that had been left untold (a species of divination always dear to poets who can so eloquently finish the interrupted words) must have felt annoyed, almost scandalized, by an audacity which leaves nothing unexpressed, nothing to be divined. If he had been called upon to express his own views upon this subject, we believe he would have confessed that in accordance with his taste, he was only permitted to give vent to his feelings on condition of suffering much to remain unrevealed, or only to be divined under the rich veils of broidery in which he wound his emotions. If that which they agree in calling classic in art appeared to him too full of methodical restrictions, if he refused to permit himself to be garroted in the manacles and frozen in the conventions of systems, if he did not like confinement although enclosed in the safe symmetry of a gilded cage, it was not because he preferred the license of disorder, the confusion of irregularity. It was rather that he might soar like the lark into the deep blue of the unclouded heavens. Like the Bird of Paradise, which it was once thought never slept but while resting upon extended wing, rocked only by the breath of unlimited space at the sublime height at which it reposed; he obstinately refused to descend to bury himself in the misty gloom of the forests, or to surround himself with the howlings and wailings with which it is filled. He would not leave the depths of azure for the wastes of the desert, or attempt to fix pathways over the treacherous waves of sand, which the winds, in exulting irony, delight to sweep over the traces of the rash mortal seeking to mark the line of his wandering through the drifting, blinding swells.

That style of Italian art which is so open, so glaring, so devoid of the attraction of mystery or of science, with all that which in German art bears the seal of vulgar, though powerful energy, was distasteful to him. Apropos of Schubert he once remarked:

"that the sublime is desecrated when followed by the trivial or commonplace." Among the composers for the piano Hummel was one of the authors whom he reread with the most pleasure. Mozart was in his eyes the ideal type, the Poet par excellence, because he, less rarely than any other author, condescended to descend the steps leading from the beautiful to the commonplace. The father of Mozart after having been present at a representation of *Idoménée* made to his son the following reproach: "You have been wrong in putting in it nothing for the long ears." It was precisely for such omissions that Chopin admired him. The gayety of Papageno charmed him; the love of Tamino with its mysterious trials seemed to him worthy of having occupied Mozart; he understood the vengeance of Donna Anna because it cast but a deeper shade upon her mourning. Yet such was his Sybaritism of purity, his dread of the commonplace, that even in this immortal work he discovered some passages whose introduction we have heard him regret. His worship for Mozart was not diminished but only saddened by this. He could sometimes forget that which was repulsive to him, but to reconcile himself to it was impossible. He seemed to be governed in this by one of those implacable and irrational instincts, which no persuasion, no effort, can ever conquer sufficiently to obtain a state of mere indifference towards the objects of the antipathy; an aversion sometimes so insurmountable, that we can only account for it by supposing it to proceed from some innate and peculiar idiosyncrasy.

After he had finished his studies in harmony with Professor Joseph Elsner, who taught him the rarely known and difficult task of being exacting towards himself, and placing the just value upon the advantages which are only to be obtained by dint of patience and labor; and after he had finished his collegiate course, it was the desire of his parents that he should travel in order that he might become familiar with the finest works under the advantage of their perfect execution. For this purpose he visited many of the German cities. He had left Warsaw upon one of these short excursions, when the revolution of the 29th of November broke out in 1830.

Forced to remain in Vienna, he was heard there in some concerts, but the Viennese public, generally so cultivated, so prompt to seize the most delicate shades of execution, the finest subtleties of thought, during this winter were disturbed and abstracted. The young artist did not produce there the effect he had the right to anticipate. He left Vienna with the design of going to London, but he came first to Paris, where he intended to remain but a short time. Upon his passport drawn up for England, he had caused to be inserted: "passing through Paris." These words sealed his fate. Long years afterwards, when he seemed not only acclimated, but naturalized in France, he would smilingly say: I am "passing through Paris."

He gave several concerts after his arrival in Paris, where he was immediately received and admired in the circles of the elite, as well as welcomed by the young artists. We remember his first appearance in the saloons of Pleyel, where the most enthusiastic and redoubled applause seemed scarcely sufficient to express our enchantment for the genius which had revealed new phases of poetic feeling, and made such happy yet bold innovations in the form of musical art.

Unlike the greater part of young débutants, he was not intoxicated or dazzled for a moment by his triumph, but accepted it without pride or false modesty, evincing none of the puerile enjoyment of gratified vanity exhibited by the *parvenus* of success. His countrymen who were then in Paris gave him a most affectionate reception. He was intimate in the house of Prince Czartoryski, of the Countess Plater, of Madame de Komar, and in that of her daughters, the Princess de Beauveau and the Countess Delphine Potocka, whose beauty, together with her indescribable and spiritual grace, made her one of the most admired sovereigns of the society of Paris. He dedicated to her his second Concerto, which contains the Adagio we have already described. The ethereal beauty of the Countess, her enchanting voice enchained him by a fascination full of respectful admiration. Her voice was destined to be the last which should vibrate upon the musician's heart. Perhaps the sweetest sounds of earth accompanied the parting soul until they blended in his ear with the first chords of the angels' lyres.

He mingled much with the Polish circle in Paris; with Orda who seemed born to command the future, and who was however killed in Algiers at twenty years of age; with Counts Plater,

Grzymala, Ostrowski, Szembeck, with Prince Lubomirski, etc. etc. As the Polish families who came afterwards to Paris were all anxious to form acquaintance with him, he continued to mingle principally with his own people. He remained through them not only *au courant* of all that was passing in his own country, but even in a kind of musical correspondence with it. He liked those who visited Paris to show him the airs or new songs they had brought with them, and when the words of these airs pleased him, he frequently wrote a new melody for them, thus popularizing them rapidly in his country although the name of their author was often unknown. The number of these melodies, due to the inspiration of the heart alone, having become considerable, he often thought of collecting them for publication. But he thought of it too late, and they remain scattered and dispersed, like the perfume of the scented flowers blessing the wilderness and sweetening the "desert air" around some wandering traveller, whom chance may have led upon their secluded track. During our stay in Poland we heard some of the melodies which are attributed to him, and which are truly worthy of him; but who would now dare to make an uncertain selection between the inspirations of the national poet, and the dreams of his people?

Chopin kept for a long time aloof from the celebrities of Paris; their glittering train repelled him. As his character and habits had more true originality than apparent eccentricity, he inspired less curiosity than they did. Besides he had sharp repartees for those who imprudently wished to force him into a display of his musical abilities. Upon one occasion after he had just left the dining-room, an indiscreet host, who had had the simplicity to promise his guests some piece executed by him as a rare dessert, pointed to him an open piano. He should have remembered that in counting without the host, it is necessary to count twice. Chopin at first refused, but wearied at last by continued persecution, assuming, to sharpen the sting of his words, a stifled and languid tone of voice, he exclaimed: "Ah, sir, I have scarcely dined!"

CHAPTER VII.

Madame Sand—Lélia—Visit to Majorca—Exclusive Ideals

IN 1836 Madame Sand had not only published *Indiana, Valentine,* and *Jacques,* but also *Lélia,* that prose poem of which she afterwards said: "If I regret having written it, it is because I could not now write it. Were I in the same state of mind now as when it was written, it would indeed be a great consolation to me to be able to commence it." The mere painting of romances in cold water colors must have seemed, without doubt, dull to Madame Sand, after having handled the hammer and chisel of the sculptor so boldly, in modeling the grand lines of that semi-colossal statue, in cutting those sinewy muscles, which even in their statuesque immobility, are full of bewildering and seductive charm. Should we continue long to gaze upon it, it excites the most painful emotion. In strong contrast to the miracle of Pygmalion, Lélia seems a living Galatea, rich in feeling, full of love, whom the deeply enamored artist has tried to bury alive in his exquisitely sculptured marble, stifling the palpitating breath, and congealing the warm blood in the vain hope of elevating and immortalizing the beauty he adores. In the presence of this vivid nature petrified by art, we cannot feel that admiration is kindled into love, but, saddened and chilled, we are forced to acknowledge that love may be frozen into mere admiration.

Brown and olive-hued Lélia! Dark as Lara, despairing as Manfred, rebellious as Cain, thou hast ranged through the depths of solitude! But thou art more ferocious, more savage, more inconsolable than they, because thou hast never found a man's heart sufficiently feminine to love thee as they were loved, to pay the homage of a confiding and blind submission to thy virile charms, to offer thee a mute yet ardent devotion, to suffer its obedience to be protected by thy Amazonian force! Woman-hero! Like the Amazons, thou hast been valiant and eager for combats; like them thou hast not feared to expose the exquisite loveliness of thy face to the fierceness of the summer's sun, or the sharp blasts of winter! Thou hast hardened thy fragile limbs by the endurance of fatigue, thus robbing them of the subtle power of their weakness! Thou hast covered thy palpitating breast with a heavy cuirass, which has pressed and torn it, dyeing its snow in blood;—that gentle woman's bosom, charming as life, discreet as the grave, which is always adored by man when his heart is permitted to form its sole, its impenetrable buckler!

After having blunted her chisel in polishing this statue, which, by its majesty, its haughty disdain, its look of hopeless anguish, shadowed by the frowning of the pure brows and by the long loose locks shivering with electric life, reminds us of those antique cameos on which we still admire the perfect features, the beautiful yet fatal brow, the haughty smile of the Medusa, whose gaze paralyzed and stopped the pulses of the human heart;—Madame Sand in vain sought another form for the expression of the emotions which tortured her insatiate soul. After having draped this figure with the highest art, accumulating every species of masculine greatness upon it in order to compensate for the highest of all qualities which she repudiated for it, the grandeur of "utter self-abnegation for love," which the many-sided poet has placed in the empyrean and called "the Eternal Feminine," (*das Ewigweibliche,*)—a greatness which is love existing before any of its joys, surviving all its sorrows;—after having caused Don Juan to be cursed, and a divine hymn to be chanted to Desire by Lélia, who, as well as Don Juan, had repulsed the only delight which crowns desire, the luxury of self-abnegation,—after having fully revenged Elvira by the creation of Stenio,—after having scorned man more than Don Juan had degraded woman,—Madame Sand, in her *Lettres d'un voyageur,* depicts the shivering palsy, the painful lethargy which seizes the artist, when, having incorporated the emotion which inspired him in his work, his imagination still remains under the domination of the insatiate idea without being able to find

another form in which to incarnate it. Such poetic sufferings
were well understood by Byron, when he makes Tasso shed his
most bitter tears, not for his chains, not for his physical sufferings, not for the ignominy heaped upon him, but for his finished
Epic, for the ideal world created by his thought and now about
to close its doors upon him, and by thus expelling him from its
enchanted realm, rendering him at last sensible of the gloomy
realities around him:—

> "But this is o'er—my pleasant task is done:—
> My long-sustaining friend of many years:
> If I do blot thy final page with tears,
> Know that my sorrows have wrung from me none.
> But thou, my young creation! my soul's child!
> Which ever playing round me came and smiled,
> And woo'd me from myself with thy sweet sight,
> Thou too art gone—and so is my delight."
>
> *Lament of Tasso.*—Byron.

At this epoch, Madame Sand often heard a musician, one of
the friends who had greeted Chopin with the most enthusiastic
joy upon his arrival at Paris, speak of him. She heard him praise
his poetic genius even more than his artistic talent. She was
acquainted with his compositions, and admired their graceful
tenderness. She was struck by the amount of emotion displayed
in his poems, with the effusions of a heart so noble and dignified. Some of the countrymen of Chopin spoke to her of the
women of their country, with the enthusiasm natural to them
upon that subject, an enthusiasm then very much increased by
a remembrance of the sublime sacrifices made by them during
the last war. Through their recitals and the poetic inspiration of
the Polish artist, she perceived an ideal of love which took the
form of worship for woman. She thought that guaranteed from
dependence, preserved from inferiority, her rôle might be like
the fairy power of the Peri, that ethereal intelligence and friend
of man. Perhaps she did not fully understand what innumerable
links of suffering, of silence, of patience, of gentleness, of indulgence, of courageous perseverance, had been necessary for the
formation of the worship for this imperious but resigned ideal,
beautiful indeed, but sad to behold, like those plants with the

rose-colored corollas, whose stems, intertwining and interlacing in a network of long and numerous branches, give life to ruins; destined ever to embellish decay, growing upon old walls and hiding only tottering stones! Beautiful veils woven by beneficent Nature, in her ingenious and inexhaustible richness, to cover the constant decay of human things!

As Madame Sand perceived that this artist, in place of giving body to his phantasy in porphyry and marble, or defining his thoughts by the creation of massive caryatides, rather effaced the contour of his works, and, had it been necessary, could have elevated his architecture itself from the soil, to suspend it, like the floating palaces of the Fata Morgana, in the fleecy clouds, through his aerial forms of almost impalpable buoyancy, she was more and more attracted by that mystic ideal which she perceived glowing within them. Though her arm was powerful enough to have sculptured the round shield, her hand was delicate enough to have traced those light relievos where the shadows of ineffaceable profiles have been thrown upon and trusted to a stone scarcely raised from its level plane. She was no stranger in the supernatural world, she to whom Nature, as to a favored child, had unloosed her girdle and unveiled all the caprices, the attractions, the delights, which she can lend to beauty. She was not ignorant of the lightest graces; she whose eye could embrace such vast proportions, had stooped to study the glowing illuminations painted upon the wings of the fragile butterfly. She had traced the symmetrical and marvellous network which the fern extends as a canopy over the wood strawberry; she had listened to the murmuring of streams through the long reeds and stems of the water-grass, where the hissing of the "amorous viper" may be heard; she had followed the wild leaps of the Will-with-a-wisp as it bounds over the surface of the meadows and marshes; she had pictured to herself the chimerical dwelling-places toward which it perfidiously attracts the benighted traveller; she had listened to the concerts given by the Cicada and their friends in the stubble of the fields; she had learned the names of the inhabitants of the winged republics of the woods which she could distinguish as well by their plumaged robes, as by their jeering roulades or plaintive cries. She knew the secret tenderness of the lily in the splendor of its tints; she had listened to the sighs of Geneviève,° the maiden enamored of flowers.

She was visited in her dreams by those "unknown friends" who came to rejoin her "when she was seized with distress upon a desolate shore," brought by a "rapid stream . . . in large and full bark" . . . upon which she mounted to leave the unknown shores, "the country of chimeras which make real life appear like a dream half effaced to those, who enamored from their infancy of large shells of pearl, mount them to land in those isles where all are young and beautiful . . . where the men and women are crowned with flowers, with their long locks floating upon their shoulders . . . holding vases and harps of a strange form . . . having songs and voices not of this world . . . all loving each other equally with a divine love . . . where crystal fountains of perfumed waters play in basins of silver . . . where blue roses bloom in vases of alabaster . . . where the perspectives are all enchanted . . . where they walk with naked feet upon the thick green moss, soft as carpets of velvet . . . where all sing as they wander among the fragrant groves."†

She knew these unknown friends so well that after having again seen them, "she could not dream of them without palpitations of the heart during the whole day." She was initiated into the Hoffmannic world—"she who had surprised such ineffable smiles upon the portraits of the dead";‡ who had seen the rays of the sun falling through the stained glass of a Gothic window form a halo round loved heads, like the arm of God, luminous and impalpable, surrounded by a vortex of atoms;—she who had known such glorious apparitions, clothed with the purple and golden glories of the setting sun. The realm of fantasy had no myth with whose secret she was not familiar!

Thus she was naturally anxious to become acquainted with one who had with rapid wing flown "to those scenes which it is impossible to describe, but which must exist somewhere, either upon the earth, or in some of the planets, whose light we love to

---

°*André.*
†*Lettres d'un voyageur.*
‡*Spiridson.*

gaze upon in the forests when the moon has set."° Such scenes
she had prayed never to be forced to desert—never desiring to
bring her heart and imagination back to this dreary world, too
like the gloomy coasts of Finland, where the slime and miry
slough can only be escaped by scaling the naked granite of the
solitary rocks. Fatigued with the massive statue she had sculptured, the Amazonian Lélia; wearied with the grandeur of an
Ideal which it is impossible to mould from the gross materials of
this earth; she was desirous to form an acquaintance with the
artist "the lover of an impossible so shadowy"—so near the starry
regions. Alas! if these regions are exempt from the poisonous
miasmas of our atmosphere, they are not free from its desolating melancholy! Perhaps those who are transported there may
adore the shining of new suns—but there are others not less
dear whose light they must see extinguished! Will not the most
glorious among the beloved constellation of the Pleiades there
disappear? Like drops of luminous dew the stars fall one by one
into the nothingness of a yawning abyss, whose bottomless
depths no plummet has ever sounded, while the soul, contemplating these fields of ether, this blue Sahara with its wandering
and perishing oases,—is stricken by a grief so hopeless, so profound, that neither enthusiasm nor love can ever soothe it more.
It ingulfs and absorbs all emotions, being no more agitated by
them than the sleeping waters of some tranquil lake, reflecting
the moving images thronging its banks from its polished surface,
are by the varied motions and eager life of the many objects mir-
rored upon its glassy bosom. The drowsy waters cannot thus be
wakened from their icy lethargy. This melancholy saddens even
the highest joy. "Through the exhaustion always accompanying
such tension, when the soul is strained above the region which
it naturally inhabits . . . the insufficiency of speech is felt for the
first time by those who have studied it so much, and used it so
well—we are borne from all active, from all militant instincts—
to travel through boundless space—to be lost in the immensity
of adventurous courses far, far above the clouds . . . where we no

---

°*Lettres d'un voyageur.*

longer see that the earth is beautiful, because our gaze is riveted upon the skies . . . where reality is no longer poetically draped, as has been so skillfully done by the author of Waverley, but where, in idealizing poetry itself, the infinite is peopled with the spirits belonging only to its mystic realm, as has been done by Byron in his Manfred."

Could Madame Sand have divined the incurable melancholy, the will which cannot blend with that of others, the imperious exclusiveness, which invariably seize upon imaginations delighting in the pursuit of dreams whose realities are nowhere to be found, or at least never in the matter-of-fact world in which the dreamers are constrained to dwell? Had she foreseen the form which devoted attachment assumes for such dreamers; had she measured the entire and absolute absorption which they will alone accept as the synonyme of tenderness? It is necessary to be in some degree shy, shrinking, and secretive as they themselves are, to be able to understand the hidden depths of characters so concentrated. Like those susceptible flowers which close their sensitive petals before the first breath of the North wind, they too veil their exacting souls in the shrouds of self concentration, unfolding themselves only under the warming rays of a propitious sun. Such natures have been called "rich by exclusiveness"; in opposition to those which are "rich by expansiveness." "If these differing temperaments should meet and approach each other, they can never mingle or melt the one into the other," (says the writer whom we have so often quoted) "but the one must consume the other, leaving nothing but ashes behind." Alas! it is the natures like that of the fragile musician whose days we commemorate, which, consuming themselves, perish; not wishing, not indeed being able, to live any life but one in conformity with their own exclusive Ideal.

Chopin seemed to dread Madame Sand more than any other woman, the modern Sibyl, who, like the Pythoness of old, had said so many things that others of her sex neither knew nor dared to say. He avoided and put off all introduction to her. Madame Sand was ignorant of this. In consequence of that captivating simplicity, which is one of her noblest charms, she did not divine his fear of the Delphic priestess. At last she was presented to him, and an acquaintance with her soon dissipated the prejudices which he had obstinately nourished against female authors.

In the fall of 1837, Chopin was attacked by an alarming illness, which left him almost without force to support life. Dangerous symptoms forced him to go South to avoid the rigor of winter. Madame Sand, always so watchful over those whom she loved, so full of compassion for their sufferings, would not permit him, when his health required so much care, to set out alone, and determined to accompany him. They selected the island of Majorca for their residence because the air of the sea, joined to the mild climate which prevails there, is especially salubrious for those who are suffering from affections of the lungs. Though he was so weak when he left Paris that we had no hope of his ever returning; though after his arrival in Majorca he was long and dangerously ill; yet so much was he benefited by the change that his health was improved during several years.

Was it the effect of the balmy climate alone which recalled him to health? Was it not rather because his life was full of bliss that he found strength to live? Did he not regain strength only because he now wished to live? Who can tell how far the influence of the will extends over the body? Who knows what internal subtle aroma it has the power of disengaging to preserve the sinking frame from decay; what vital force it can breathe into the debilitated organs? Who can say where the dominion of mind over matter ceases? Who knows how far our senses are under the dominion of the imagination, to what extent their powers may be increased, or their extinction accelerated, by its influence? It matters not how the imagination gains its strange extension of power, whether through long and bitter exercise, or, whether spontaneously collecting its forgotten strength, it concentrates its force in some new and decisive moment of destiny: as when the rays of the sun are able to kindle a flame of celestial origin when concentrated in the focus of the burning glass, brittle and fragile though the medium be.

All the long scattered rays of happiness were collected within this epoch of the life of Chopin; is it then surprising that they should have rekindled the flame of life, and that it should have burned at this time with the most vivid lustre? The solitude surrounded by the blue waves of the Mediterranean and shaded by

groves of orange, seemed fitted in its exceeding loveliness for
the ardent vows of youthful lovers, still believing in their naïve
and sweet illusions, sighing for happiness in "some desert isle."
He breathed there that air for which natures unsuited for the
world, and never feeling themselves happy in it, long with such
a painful home-sickness; that air which may be found everywhere if we can find the sympathetic souls to breathe it with us,
and which is to be met nowhere without them; that air of the
land of our dreams; and which in spite of all obstacles, of the bitter real, is easily discovered when sought by two! It is the air of
the country of the ideal to which we gladly entice the being we
cherish, repeating with poor Mignon: *Dahin! dahin! . . . lasst
uns ziehn!*

As long as his sickness lasted, Madame Sand never left the pillow of him who loved her even to death, with an attachment
which in losing all its joys, did not lose its intensity, which
remained faithful to her even after all its memories had turned
to pain: "for it seemed as if this fragile being was absorbed and
consumed by the strength of his affection. . . . Others seek happiness in their attachments; when they no longer find it, the
attachment gently vanishes. In this they resemble the rest of the
world. But he loved for the sake of loving. No amount of suffering was sufficient to discourage him. He could enter upon a new
phase, that of woe; but the phase of coldness he could never
arrive at. It would have been indeed a phase of physical agony—
for his love was his life—and delicious or bitter, he had not the
power of withdrawing himself a single moment from its domination."* Madame Sand never ceased to be for Chopin that
being of magic spells who had snatched him from the valley of
the shadow of death, whose power had changed his physical
agony into the delicious languor of love.

To save him from death, to bring him back to life, she strug-
gled courageously with his disease. She surrounded him with
those divining and instinctive cares which are a thousand times
more efficacious than the material remedies known to science.

Lucrezia Floriana.

While engaged in nursing him, she felt no fatigue, no weariness, no discouragement. Neither her strength, nor her patience, yielded before the task. Like the mothers in robust health, who appear to communicate a part of their own strength to the sickly infant who, constantly requiring their care, have also their preference, she nursed the precious charge into new life. The disease yielded: "the funereal oppression which secretly undermined the spirit of Chopin, destroying and corroding all contentment, gradually vanished. He permitted the amiable character, the cheerful serenity of his friend to chase sad thoughts and mournful presentiments away, and to breathe new force into his intellectual being."

Happiness succeeded to gloomy fears, like the gradual progression of a beautiful day after a night full of obscurity and terror, when so dense and heavy is the vault of darkness which weighs upon us from above, that we are prepared for a sudden and fatal catastrophe, we do not even dare to dream of deliverance, when the despairing eye suddenly catches a bright spot where the mists clear, and the clouds open like flocks of heavy wool yielding, even while the edges thicken under the pressure of the hand which rends them. At this moment, the first ray of hope penetrates the soul. We breathe more freely like those who lost in the windings of a dark cavern at last think they see a light, though indeed its existence is still doubtful. This faint light is the day dawn, though so colorless are its rays, that it is more like the extinction of the dying twilight,—the fall of the night-shroud upon the earth. But it is indeed the dawn; we know it by the vivid and pure breath of the young zephyrs which it sends forth, like avant-coureurs, to bear us the assurance of morn and safety. The balm of flowers fills the air, like the thrilling of an encouraged hope. A stray bird accidentally commences his song earlier than usual, it soothes the heart like a distant consolation, and is accepted as a promise for the future. As the imperceptibly progressive but sure indications multiply, we are convinced that in this struggle of light and darkness it is the shadows of night which are to yield. Raising our eyes to the Dome of lead above us, we feel that it weighs less heavily upon us, that it has already lost its fatal stability.

Little by little the long gray lines of light increase, they stretch
themselves along the horizon like fissures into a brighter world.
They suddenly enlarge, they gain upon their dark boundaries,
now they break through them, as the waters bounding the edge
of a lake inundate in irregular pools the arid banks. Then a
fierce opposition begins, banks and long dikes accumulate to
arrest the progress. The clouds are oiled like ridges of sand,
tossing and surging to present obstructions, but like the impetuous raging of irresistible waters, the light breaks through them,
demolishes them, devours them, and as the rays ascend, the
rolling waves of purple mist glow into crimson. At this moment
the young dawn shines with a timid yet victorious grace, while
the knee bends in admiration and gratitude before it, for the last
terror has vanished, and we feel as if new born.

Fresh objects strike upon the view, as if just called from
chaos. A veil of uniform rose-color covers them all, but as the
light augments in intensity, the thin gauze drapes and folds in
shades of pale carnation, while the advancing plains grow clear
in white and dazzling splendor.

The brilliant sun delays no longer to invade the firmament,
gaining new glory as he rises. The vapors surge and crowd
together, rolling themselves from right to left, like the heavy
drapery of a curtain moved by the wind. Then all breathes,
moves, lives, hums, sings; the sounds mingle, cross, meet, and
melt into each other. Inertia gives place to motion, it spreads,
accelerates and circulates. The waves of the lake undulate and
swell like a bosom touched by love. The tears of the dew,
motionless as those of tenderness, grow more and more percep-
tible, one after another they are seen glittering on the humid
herbs, diamonds waiting for the sun to paint with rainbow-tints
their vivid scintillations. The gigantic fan of light in the East is
ever opening larger and wider. Spangles of silver, borders of
scarlet, violet fringes, bars of gold, cover it with fantastic broidery. Light bands of reddish brown feather its branches. The
brightest scarlet at its centre has the glowing transparency of the
ruby; shading into orange like a burning coal, it widens like a
torch, spreads like a bouquet of flames, which glows and glows
from fervor to fervor, ever more incandescent.

At last the god of day appears! His blazing front is adorned with luminous locks of long floating hair. Slowly he seems to rise—but scarcely has he fully unveiled himself, than he starts forward, disengages himself from all around him, and, leaving the earth far below him, takes instantaneous possession of the vaulted heavens . . .

The memory of the days passed in the lovely isle of Majorca, like the remembrance of an entrancing ecstasy, which fate grants but once in life even to the most favored of her children, remained always dear to the heart of Chopin. "He° was no longer upon this earth, he was in an empyrean of golden clouds and perfumes, his imagination, so full of exquisite beauty, seemed engaged in a monologue with God himself; and if upon the radiant prism in whose contemplation he forgot all else, the magic-lantern of the outer world would even cast its disturbing shadow, he felt deeply pained, as if in the midst of a sublime concert, a shrieking old woman should blend her shrill yet bro- ken tones, her vulgar musical motivo, with the divine thoughts of the great masters." He always spoke of this period with deep emotion, profound gratitude, as if its happiness had been suffi- cient for a life-time, without hoping that it would ever be possi- ble again to find a felicity in which the fight of time was only marked by the tenderness of woman's love, and the brilliant flashes of true genius. Thus did the clock of Linnaeus mark the course of time, indicating the hours by the successive waking and sleeping of the flowers, marking each by a different per- fume, and a display of ever varying beauties, as each variegated calyx opened in ever changing yet ever lovely form!

The beauties of the countries through which the Poet and Musician travelled together, struck with more distinctness the imagination of the former. The loveliness of nature impressed Chopin in a manner less definite, though not less strong. His soul was touched, and immediately harmonized with the exter- nal enchantment, yet his intellect did not feel the necessity of analyzing or classifying it. His heart vibrated in unison with the

---

°*Lucrezia Floriana.*

exquisite scenery around him, although he was not able at the
moment to assign the precise source of his blissful tranquillity.
Like a true musician, he was satisfied to seize the sentiment of
the scenes he visited, while he seemed to give but little attention to the plastic material, the picturesque frame, which did
not assimilate with the form of his art, nor belong to his more
spiritualized sphere. However, (a fact that has been often
remarked in organizations such as his) as he was removed in
time and distance from the scenes in which emotion had
obscured his senses, as the clouds from the burning incense
envelope the censer, the more vividly the forms and beauties of
such scenes stood out in his memory. In the succeeding years,
he frequently spoke of them, as though the remembrance was
full of pleasure to him. But when so entirely happy, he made no
inventory of his bliss. He enjoyed it simply, as we all do in the
sweet years of childhood, when we are deeply impressed by the
scenery surrounding us without ever thinking of its details, yet
finding, long after, the exact image of each object in our memory, though we are only able to describe its forms when we have
ceased to behold them.

Besides, why should he have tasked himself to scrutinize the
beautiful sites in Spain which formed the appropriate setting of
his poetic happiness? Could he not always find them again
through the descriptions of his inspired companion? As all
objects, even the atmosphere itself, become flame-colored
when seen through a glass dyed in crimson, so he might contemplate these delicious sites in the glowing hues cast around
them by the impassioned genius of the woman he loved. The
nurse of his sick-room—was she not also a great artist? Rare and
beautiful union! If to the depths of tenderness and devotion, in
which the true and irresistible empire of woman must commence, and deprived of which she is only an enigma without a
possible solution, nature should unite the most brilliant gifts of
genius,—the miraculous spectacle of the Greek fire would be
renewed,—the glittering flames would again sport over the
abysses of the ocean without being extinguished or submerged
in the chilling depths, adding, as the living hues were thrown

upon the surging waves, the glowing dyes of the purple fire to the celestial blue of the heaven-reflecting sea!

Has genius ever attained that utter self-abnegation, that sublime humility of heart which gives the power to make those strange sacrifices of the entire Past, of the whole Future; those immolations, as courageous as mysterious; those mystic and utter holocausts of self, not temporary and changing, but monotonous and constant,—through whose might alone tenderness may justly claim the higher name, devotion? Has not the force of genius its own exclusive and legitimate exactions, and does not the force of woman consist in the abdication of all exactions? Can the royal purple and burning flames of genius ever float upon the immaculate azure of woman's destiny? . . .

CHAPTER VIII.

FROM the date of 1840, the health of Chopin, affected by so
many changes, visibly declined. During some years, his
most tranquil hours were spent at Nohant, where he seemed to
suffer less than elsewhere. He composed there, with pleasure,
bringing with him every year to Paris several new compositions,
but every winter caused him an increase of suffering. Motion
became at first difficult, and soon almost impossible to him.
From 1846 to 1847, he scarcely walked at all; he could not
ascend the staircase without the most painful sensation of suffo-
cation, and his life was only prolonged through continual care
and the greatest precaution.

Towards the Spring of 1847, as his health grew more precarious from day to day, he was attacked by an illness from which it
was thought he could never recover. He was saved for the last
time; but this epoch was marked by an event so agonizing to his
heart that he immediately called it mortal. Indeed, he did not
long survive the rupture of his friendship with Madame Sand,
which took place at this date. Madame de Staël, who, in spite of
her generous and impassioned heart, her subtle and vivid intellect, fell sometimes into the fault of making her sentences heavy
through a species of pedantry which robbed them of the grace
of "abandon," remarked on one of those occasions when the
strength of her feelings made her forget the solemnity of her
Genevese stiffness: "In affection, there are only beginnings!"
This exclamation was based upon the bitter experience of the
insufficiency of the human heart to accomplish the beautiful
and blissful dreams of the imagination. Ah! if some blessed
examples of human devotion did not sometimes occur to con-

tradict the melancholy words of Madame de Staël, which so many illustrious as well as obscure facts seem to prove, our suspicions might lead us to be guilty of much ingratitude and want of trust; we might be led to doubt the sincerity of the hearts which surround us, and see but the allegorical symbols of human affections in the antique train of the beautiful Canephoroe, who carried the fragile and perfumed flowers to adorn some hapless victim for the altar!

Chopin spoke frequently and almost by preference of Madame Sand, without bitterness or recrimination. Tears always filled his eyes when he named her; but with a kind of bitter sweetness he gave himself up to the memories of past days, alas, now stripped of their manifold significance! In spite of the many subterfuges employed by his friends to entice him from dwelling upon remembrances which always brought dangerous excitement with them, he loved to return to them; as if through the same feelings which had once reanimated his life, he now wished to destroy it, sedulously stifling its powers through the vapor of this subtle poison. His last pleasure seemed to be the memory of the blasting of his last hope; he treasured the bitter knowledge that under this fatal spell his life was ebbing fast away. All attempts to fix his attention upon other objects were made in vain, he refused to be comforted and would constantly speak of the one engrossing subject. Even if he had ceased to speak of it, would he not always have thought of it? He seemed to inhale the poison rapidly and eagerly, that he might thus shorten the time in which he would be forced to breathe it!

Although the exceeding fragility of his physical constitution might not have allowed him, under any circumstances, to have lingered long on earth, yet at least he might have been spared the bitter sufferings which clouded his last hours! With a tender and ardent soul, though exacting through its fastidiousness and excessive delicacy, he could not live unless surrounded by the radiant phantoms he had himself evoked; he could not expel the profound sorrow which his heart cherished as the sole remaining fragment of the happy past. He was another great and illustrious victim to the transitory attachments occurring between

persons of different character, who, experiencing a surprise full
of delight in their first sudden meeting, mistake it for a durable
feeling, and build hopes and illusions upon it which can never
be realized. It is always the nature the most deeply moved, the
most absolute in its hopes and attachments, for which all trans-
plantation is impossible, which is destroyed and ruined in the
painful awakening from the absorbing dream! Terrible power
exercised over man by the most exquisite gifts which he possesses! Like the coursers of the sun, when the hand of Phæton,
in place of guiding their beneficent career, permits them to
wander at random, disordering the beautiful structure of the
celestial spheres, they bring devastation and flames in their
train! Chopin felt and often repeated that the sundering of this
long friendship, the rupture of this strong tie, broke all the
chords which bound him to life.

During this attack his life was despaired of for several days.
M. Gutman, his most distinguished pupil, and during the last
years of his life, his most intimate friend, lavished upon him
every proof of tender attachment. His cares, his attentions, were
the most agreeable to him. With the timidity natural to invalids,
and with the tender delicacy peculiar to himself, he once asked
the Princess Czartoryska, who visited him every day, often fear-
ing that on the morrow he would no longer be among the living:
"if Gutman was not very much fatigued? If she thought he
would be able to continue his care of him"; adding, "that his
presence was dearer to him than that of any other person." His
convalescence was very slow and painful, leaving him indeed
but the semblance of life. At this epoch he changed so much in
appearance that he could scarcely be recognized.

The next summer brought him that deceptive decrease of suffering which it sometimes grants to those who are dying. He
refused to quit Paris, and thus deprived himself of the pure air
of the country, and the benefit of this vivifying element.

The winter of 1847 to 1848 was filled with a painful and continual succession of improvements and relapses. Notwithstanding
this, he resolved in the spring to accomplish his old project of
visiting London. When the revolution of February broke out, he
was still confined to bed, but with a melancholy effort, he
seemed to try to interest himself in the events of the day, and

spoke of them more than usual. M. Gutman continued his most intimate and constant visitor. He accepted through preference his cares until the close of his life.

Feeling better in the month of April, he thought of realizing his contemplated journey, of visiting that country to which he had intended to go when youth and life opened in bright perspective before him. He set out for England, where his works had already found an intelligent public, and were generally known and admired.° He left France in that mood of mind which the English call "low spirits." The transitory interest

---

°The compositions of Chopin were, even at that time, known and very much liked in England. The most distinguished virtuosi frequently executed them. In a pamphlet published in London by Messrs. Wessel and Stappleton, under the title of *An Essay on the Works of F. Chopin,* we find some lines marked by just criticism. The epigraph of this little pamphlet is ingeniously chosen, and the two lines from Shelley could scarcely be better applied than to Chopin:

> "He was a mighty poet—and
> A subtle-souled Psychologist."

The author of this pamphlet speaks with enthusiasm of the "originative genius untrammeled by conventionalities, unfettered by pedantry; . . . of the outpourings of an unworldly and tristful soul—those musical floods of tears, and gushes of pure joyfulness—those exquisite embodiments of fugitive thoughts—those infinitesimal delicacies, which give so much value to the lightest sketch of Chopin." The English author again says: "One thing is certain, viz.: to play with proper feeling and correct execution, the *Preludes* and *Studies* of Chopin, is to be neither more nor less than a finished pianist, and moreover to comprehend them thoroughly, to give a life and tongue to their infinite and most eloquent subtleties of expression, involves the necessity of being in no less a degree a poet than a pianist, a thinker than a musician. Commonplace is instinctively avoided in all the works of Chopin; a stale cadence or a trite progression, a humdrum subject or a hackneyed sequence, a vulgar twist of the melody or a worn-out passage, a meagre harmony or an unskillful counterpoint, may in vain be looked for throughout the entire range of his compositions; the prevailing characteristics of which, are, a feeling as uncommon as beautiful, a treatment as original as felicitous, a melody and a harmony as new, fresh, vigorous, and striking, as they are utterly unexpected and out of the common track. In taking up one of the works of Chopin, you are entering, as it were, a fairy land, untrodden by human footsteps, a path hitherto unfrequented but by the great composer himself; and a faith, a devotion, a desire to appreciate and a determination to understand are absolutely necessary, to do it anything like adequate justice. . . . Chopin in his *Polonaises*

which he had endeavored to take in political changes, soon disappeared. He became more taciturn than ever. If through absence of mind, a few words would escape him, they were only exclamations of regret. His affection for the limited number of persons whom he continued to see, was filled with that heart-rending emotion which precedes eternal farewells! Art alone always retained its absolute power over him. Music absorbed him during the time, now constantly shortening, in which he was able to occupy himself with it, as completely as during the days when he was full of life and hope. Before he left Paris, he gave a concert in the saloon of M. Pleyel, one of the friends with whom his relations had been the most constant, the most frequent, and the most affectionate; who is now rendering a worthy homage to his memory, occupying himself with zeal and activity in the execution of a monument for his tomb. At this concert, his chosen and faithful audience heard him for the last time!

He was received in London with an eagerness which had some effect in aiding him to shake off his sadness, to dissipate his mournful depression. Perhaps he dreamed, by burying all his former habits in oblivion, he could succeed in dissipating his melancholy! He neglected the prescriptions of his physicians, with all the precautions which reminded him of his wretched health. He played twice in public, and many times in private concerts. He mingled much in society, sat up late at night, and exposed himself to considerable fatigue, without permitting himself to be deterred by any consideration for his health.

He was presented to the Queen by the Duchess of Sutherland, and the most distinguished society sought the pleasure of his acquaintance. He went to Edinburgh, where the climate was particularly injurious to him. He was much debilitated upon his return from Scotland; his physicians wished him to leave

---

and in his *Mazourkas* has aimed at those characteristics, which distinguish the national music of his country so markedly from, that of all others, that quaint idiosyncrasy, that identical wildness and fantasticality, that delicious mingling of the sad and cheerful, which invariably and forcibly individualize the music of those Northern nations, whose language delights in combinations of consonants. . . ."

England immediately, but he delayed for some time his departure. Who can read the feelings which caused this delay! . . . He played again at a concert given for the Poles. It was the last mark of love sent to his beloved country—the last look—the last sigh—the last regret! He was fêted, applauded, and surrounded by his own people. He bade them all adieu,—they did not know it was an eternal Farewell! What thoughts must have filled his sad soul as he crossed the sea to return to Paris! That Paris so different now for him from that which he had found without seeking in 1831!

He was met upon his arrival by a surprise as painful as unexpected. Dr. Molin, whose advice and intelligent prescriptions had saved his life in the winter of 1847, to whom alone he believed himself indebted for the prolongation of his life, was dead. He felt his loss painfully, nay, it brought a profound discouragement with it; at a time when the mind exercises so much influence over the progress of the disease, he persuaded himself that no one could replace the trusted physician, and he had no confidence in any other. Dissatisfied with them all, without any hope from their skill, he changed them constantly. A kind of superstitious depression seized him. No tie stronger than life, no love powerful as death, came now to struggle against this bitter apathy! From the winter of 1848, Chopin had been in no condition to labor continuously. From time to time he retouched some scattered leaves, without succeeding in arranging his thoughts in accordance with his designs. A respectful care of his fame dictated to him the wish that these sketches should be destroyed to prevent the possibility of their being mutilated, disfigured, and transformed into posthumous works unworthy of his hand.

He left no finished manuscripts, except a very short *Waltz,* and a last *Nocturne,* as parting memories. In the later period of his life he thought of writing a method for the Piano, in which he intended to give his ideas upon the theory and technicality of his art, the results of his long and patient studies, his happy innovations, and his intelligent experience. The task was a difficult one, demanding redoubled application even from one who labored as assiduously as Chopin. Perhaps he wished to avoid the emotions of art, (affecting those who reproduce them in

serenity of soul so differently from those who repeat in them
their own desolation of heart,) by taking refuge in a region so
barren. He sought in this employment only an absorbing and
uniform occupation, he only asked from it what Manfred
demanded in vain from the powers of magic: "forgetfulness!"
Forgetfulness—granted neither by the gayety of amusement,
nor the lethargy of torpor! On the contrary, with venomous
guile, they always compensate in the renewed intensity of woe,
for the time they may have succeeded in benumbing it. In the
daily labor which "charms the storms of the soul," *(der Seele
Sturm beschwört,)* he sought without doubt forgetfulness,
which occupation, by rendering the memory torpid, may sometimes procure, though it cannot destroy the sense of pain. At the
close of that fine elegy which he names "The Ideal," a poet, who
was also the victim of an inconsolable melancholy, appeals to
labor as a consolation when a prey to bitter regret; while expect-
ing an early death, he invokes occupation as the last resource
against the incessant anguish of life:

> "And thou, so pleased, with her uniting,
> To charm the soul-storm into peace,
> Sweet toil, in toil itself delighting,
> That more it labored, less could cease,
> Though but by grains thou aidest the pile
> The vast eternity uprears,
> At least thou strikest from *time* the while
> Life's debt—the minutes—days—and years."
> > *Bulwer's translation of* SCHILLER'S *"Ideal."*

> *Beschœftigung, die nie ermattet*
> *Die langsam schafft, doch nie zerstœrt,*
> *Die zu dem Bau der Ewigkeiten*
> *Zwar Sandkorn nur, fuer Sandkorn reicht,*
> *Doch von der grossen Schuld der Zeiten*
> *Minute, Tage, Jahre streicht.*
> > *Die Ideale—*SCHILLER.

The strength of Chopin was not sufficient for the execution of
his intention. The occupation was too abstract, too fatiguing. He
contemplated the form of his project, he spoke of it at different
times, but its execution had become impossible. He wrote but a
few pages of it, which were destroyed with the rest.

At last the disease augmented so visibly, that the fears of his friends assumed the hue of despair. He scarcely ever left his bed, and spoke but rarely. His sister, upon receiving this intelligence, came from Warsaw to take her place at his pillow, which she left no more. He witnessed the anguish, the presentiments, the redoubled sadness around him, without showing what impression they made upon him. He thought of death with Christian calm and resignation, yet he did not cease to prepare for the morrow. The fancy he had for changing his residence was once more manifested, he took another lodging, disposed the furnishing of it anew, and occupied himself in its most minute details. As he had taken no measures to recall the orders he had given for its arrangement, they were transporting his furniture to the apartments he was destined never to inhabit, upon the very day of his death!

Did he fear that death would not fulfil his plighted promise? Did he dread, that after having touched him with his icy hand, he would still suffer him to linger upon earth? Did he feel that life would be almost unendurable with its fondest ties broken, its closest links dissevered? There is a double influence often felt by gifted temperaments when upon the eve of some event which is to decide their fate. The eager heart, urged on by a desire to unravel the mystic secrets of the unknown Future, contradicts the colder, the more timid intellect, which fears to plunge into the uncertain abyss of the coming fate! This want of harmony between the simultaneous previsions of the mind and heart, often causes the firmest spirits to make assertions which their actions seem to contradict; yet actions and assertions both flow from the differing sources of an equal conviction. Did Chopin suffer from this inevitable dissimilarity between the prophetic whispers of the heart, and the thronging doubts of the questioning mind?

From week to week, and soon from day to day, the cold shadow of death gained upon him. His end was rapidly approaching; his sufferings became more and more intense; his crises grew more frequent, and at each accelerated occurrence, resembled more and more a mortal agony. He retained his presence of mind, his vivid will upon their intermission, until the last; neither losing the precision of his ideas, nor the clear perception of his intentions. The wishes which he expressed in his short moments of respite, evinced the calm solemnity with which he contemplated the approach of death. He desired to be buried by the side of Bellini, with whom, during the time of Bellini's residence in Paris, he had been intimately acquainted. The grave of Bellini is in the cemetery of Père La-Chaise, next to that of Cherubini. The desire of forming an acquaintance with this great master whom he had been brought up to admire, was one of the motives which, when he left Vienna in 1831 to go to London, induced him, without foreseeing that his destiny would fix him there, to pass through Paris. Chopin now sleeps between Bellini and Cherubini, men of very dissimilar genius, and yet to both of whom he was in an equal degree allied, as he attached as much value to the respect he felt for the science of the one, as to the sympathy he acknowledged for the creations of the other. Like the author of *Norma*, he was full of melodic feeling, yet he was ambitious of attaining the harmonic depth of the learned old master; desiring to unite, in a great and elevated style, the dreamy vagueness of spontaneous emotion with the erudition of the most consummate masters.

Continuing the reserve of his manners to the very last, he did not request to see any one for the last time; but he evinced the most touching gratitude to all who approached him. The first days of October left neither doubt nor hope. The fatal moment drew near. The next day, the next hour, could no longer be relied upon. M. Gutman and his sister were in constant attendance upon him, never for a single moment leaving him. The Countess Delphine Potocka, who was then absent from Paris, returned as soon as she was informed of his imminent danger. None of those who approached the dying artist, could tear themselves from the spectacle of this great and gifted soul in its hours of mortal anguish.

However violent or frivolous the passions may be which agitate our hearts, whatever strength or indifference may be displayed in meeting unforeseen or sudden accidents, which would seem necessarily overwhelming in their effects, it is impossible to escape the impression made by the imposing majesty of a lingering and beautiful death, which touches, softens, fascinates and elevates even the souls the least prepared for such holy and sublime emotions. The lingering and gradual departure of one among us for those unknown shores, the mysterious solemnity of his secret dreams, his commemoration of past facts and passing ideas when still breathing upon the narrow strait which separates time from eternity, affect us more deeply than anything else in this world. Sudden catastrophes, the dreadful alternations forced upon the shuddering fragile ship, tossed like a toy by the wild breath of the tempest; the blood of the battle-field, with the gloomy smoke of artillery; the horrible charnel-house into which our own habitation is converted by a contagious plague; conflagrations which wrap whole cities in their glittering flames; fathomless abysses which open at our feet;—remove us less sensibly from all the fleeting attachments "which pass, which can be broken, which cease," than the prolonged view of a soul conscious of its own position, silently contemplating the multiform aspects of time and the mute door of eternity! The courage, the resignation, the elevation, the emotion, which reconcile it with that inevitable dissolution so repugnant to all our instincts, certainly impress the bystanders more profoundly than the most frightful catastrophes, which, in the confusion they create, rob the scene of its still anguish, its solemn meditation.

The parlor adjoining the chamber of Chopin was constantly occupied by some of his friends, who, one by one, in turn, approached him to receive a sign of recognition, a look of affection, when he was no longer able to address them in words. On Sunday, the 15th of October, his attacks were more violent and more frequent—lasting for several hours in succession. He endured them with patience and great strength of mind. The Countess Delphine Potocka, who was present, was much distressed; her tears were flowing fast when he observed her standing at the foot of his bed, tall, slight, draped in white, resembling the beautiful angels created by the imagination of the most devout among the painters. Without doubt, he supposed her to be a celestial apparition; and when the crisis left him a moment in repose, he requested her to sing; they deemed him at first seized with delirium, but he eagerly repeated his request. Who could have ventured—to oppose his wish? The piano was rolled from his parlor to the door of his chamber, while, with sobs in her voice, and tears streaming down her cheeks, his gifted countrywoman sang. Certainly, this delightful voice had never before attained an expression so full of profound pathos. He seemed to suffer less as he listened. She sang that famous Canticle to the Virgin, which, it is said, once saved the life of Stradella. "How beautiful it is!" he exclaimed. "My God, how very beautiful! Again—again!" Though overwhelmed with emotion, the Countess had the noble courage to comply with the last wish of a friend, a compatriot; she again took a seat at the piano, and sung a hymn from Marcello. Chopin again feeling worse, everybody was seized with fright—by a spontaneous impulse all who were present threw themselves upon their knees—no one ventured to speak; the sacred silence was only broken by the voice of the Countess, floating, like a melody from heaven, above the sighs and sobs which formed its heavy and mournful earth-accompaniment. It was the haunted hour of twilight; a dying light lent its mysterious shadows to this sad scene—the sister of Chopin prostrated near his bed, wept and prayed—and never quitted this attitude of supplication while the life of the brother she had so cherished lasted.

His condition altered for the worse during the night, but he felt more tranquil upon Monday morning, and as if he had known in advance the appointed and propitious moment, he asked to receive immediately the last sacraments. In the absence of the Abbé ——, with whom he had been very intimate since their common expatriation, he requested that the Abbé Jelowicki, one of the most distinguished men of the Polish emigration, should be sent for. When the holy Viaticum was administered to him, he received it, surrounded by those who loved him, with great devotion. He called his friends a short time afterwards, one by one, to his bedside, to give each of them his last earnest blessing; calling down the grace of God fervently upon themselves, their affections, and their hopes,—every knee bent—every head bowed—all eyes were heavy with tears—every heart was sad and oppressed—every soul elevated.

Attacks more and more painful, returned and continued during the day; from Monday night until Tuesday, he did not utter a single word. He did not seem able to distinguish the persons who were around him. About eleven o'clock on Tuesday evening, he appeared to revive a little. The Abbé Jelowicki had never left him. Hardly had he recovered the power of speech, than he requested him to recite with him the prayers and litanies for the dying. He was able to accompany the Abbé in an audible and intelligible voice. From this moment until his death, he held his head constantly supported upon the shoulder of M. Gutman, who, during the whole course of this sickness, had devoted his days and nights to him.

A convulsive sleep lasted until the 17th of October, 1849. The final agony commenced about two o'clock; a cold sweat ran profusely from his brow; after a short drowsiness, he asked, in a voice scarcely audible: "Who is near me?" Being answered, he bent his head to kiss the hand of M. Gutman, who still supported it—while giving this last tender proof of love and gratitude, the soul of the artist left its fragile clay. He died as he had lived—in loving.

When the doors of the parlor were opened, his friends threw themselves around the loved corpse, not able to suppress the gush of tears.

His love for flowers being well known, they were brought in such quantities the next day, that the bed in which they had placed them, and indeed the whole room, almost disappeared, hidden by their varied and brilliant hues. He seemed to repose in a garden of roses. His face regained its early beauty, its purity of expression, its long unwonted serenity. Calmly—with his youthful loveliness, so long dimmed by bitter suffering, restored by death, he slept among the flowers he loved, the last long and dreamless sleep!

M. Clesinger reproduced the delicate traits, to which death had rendered their early beauty, in a sketch which he immediately modeled, and which he afterwards executed in marble for his tomb.

The respectful admiration which Chopin felt for the genius of Mozart, had induced him to request that his *Requiem* should be performed at his obsequies; this wish was complied with. The funeral ceremonies took place in the Madeleine Church, the 30th of October, 1849. They had been delayed until this date, in order that the execution of this great work should be worthy of the master and his disciple. The principal artists in Paris were anxious to take part in it. The *Funeral March* of Chopin, arranged for the instruments for this occasion by M. Reber, was introduced at the Introit. At the Offertory, M. Lefebure Vély executed his admirable *Preludes* in *si* and *mi minor* upon the organ. The solos of the *Requiem* were claimed by Madame Viardot and Madame Castellan. Lablache, who had sung the *Tuba Mirum* of this *Requiem* at the burial of Beethoven in 1827, again sung it upon this occasion. M. Meyerbeer, with Prince Adam Czartoryski, led the train of mourners. The pall was borne by M. Delacroix, M. Franchomme, M. Gutman, and Prince Alexander Czartoryski.—

However insufficient these pages may be to speak of Chopin as we would have desired, we hope that the attraction which so justly surrounds his name, will compensate for much that may be wanting in them. If to these lines, consecrated to the commemoration of his works and to all that he held dear, which the sincere esteem, enthusiastic regard, and intense sorrow for his loss, can alone gift with persuasive and sympathetic power, it were necessary to add some of the thoughts awakened in every man when death robs him of the loved cotemporaries of his youth, thus breaking the first ties linked by the confiding and deluded heart with so much the greater pain if they were strong enough to survive that bright period of young life, we would say that in the same year we have lost the two dearest friends we have known on earth. One of them perished in the wild course of civil war. Unfortunate and valiant hero! He fell with his burning courage unsubdued, his intrepid calmness undisturbed, his chivalric temerity unabated, through the endurance of the horrible tortures of a fearful death. He was a Prince of rare intelligence, of great activity, of eminent faculties, through whose veins the young blood circulated with the glittering ardor of a subtle gas. By his own indefatigable energy he had just succeeded in removing the difficulties which obstructed his path, in creating an arena in which his faculties might have displayed themselves with as much success in debates and the management of civil affairs, as they had already done in brilliant feats in arms. The other, Chopin, died slowly, consuming himself in the flames of his own genius. His life, unconnected with public events, was like some fact which has never been incorporated in a material body. The traces of his existence are only to be found in the works which he has left. He ended his days upon a foreign soil, which he never considered as his country, remaining faithful in the devotion of his affections to the eternal widowhood of his own. He was a Poet of a mournful soul, full of reserve and complicated mystery, and familiar with the stern face of sorrow.

The immediate interest which we felt in the movements of the parties to which the life of Prince Felix Lichnowsky was bound, was broken by his death: the death of Chopin has robbed us of all the consolations of an intelligent and comprehensive friendship. The affectionate sympathy with our feelings, with our manner of understanding art, of which this exclusive artist has given us so many proofs, would have softened the disappointment and weariness which yet await us, and have strengthened us in our earliest tendencies, confirmed us in our first essays.

Since it has fallen to our lot to survive them, we wish at least to express the sincere regret we feel for their loss. We deem ourselves bound to offer the homage of our deep and respectful sorrow upon the grave of the remarkable musician who has just passed from among us. Music is at present receiving such great and general development, that it reminds us of that which took place in painting in the fourteenth and fifteenth centuries. Even the artists who limited the productions of their genius to the margins of parchments, painted their miniatures with an inspiration so happy, that having broken through the Byzantine stiffness, they left the most exquisite types, which the Francias, the Peruginos, and the Raphaels to come were to transport to their frescos, and introduce upon their canvas.

———

There have been people among whom, in order to preserve the memory of their great men or the signal events of their history, it was the custom to form pyramids composed of the stones which each passer-by was expected to bring to the pile, which gradually increased to an unlooked-for height from the anonymous contributions of all. Monuments are still in our days erected by an analogous proceeding, but in place of building only a rude and unformed hillock, in consequence of a fortunate combination the contribution of all concurs in the creation of some work of art, which is not only destined to perpetuate the mute remembrance which they wish to honor, but which may have the power to awaken in future ages the feelings which gave birth to such creation, the emotions of the cotemporaries which called it into being. The subscriptions which are opened to raise statues and noble memorials to those who have rendered their epoch or country illustrious, originate in this design. Immediately after the death of Chopin, M. Camille Pleyel conceived a project of this kind. He commenced a subscription, (which conformably to the general expectation rapidly amounted to a considerable sum,) to have the monument modeled by M. Clesinger, executed in marble and placed in the Père La-Chaise. In thinking over our long friendship with Chopin; on the exceptional admiration which we have always felt for him ever since his appearance in the musical world; remembering that, artist like himself, we have been the frequent interpreter of his inspirations, an interpreter, we may safely venture to say, loved and chosen by himself; that we have more frequently than others received from his own lips the spirit of his style; that we were in some degree identified with his creations in art, and with the feelings which he confided to it, through that long and constant assimilation which obtains between a writer and his translator;—we have fondly thought that these connective circumstances imposed upon us a higher and nearer duty than that of merely adding an unformed and anonymous stone to the growing pyramid of homage which his cotemporaries are elevating to him. We believed that the claims of a tender friendship for our illustrious colleague, exacted from us a more particular expression of our profound regret, of our high admiration. It appeared to us that we would not be true to ourselves, did we not court the honor of inscribing our name, our deep affliction, upon his sepulchral stone! This should be granted to those who never hope to fill the void in their hearts left by an irreparable loss! . . .